STEP-BY-STEP
cakes

STEP-BY-STEP
cakes

Caroline Bretherton

Content previously published in *Illustrated Step-by-Step Baking*

LONDON, NEW YORK,
MUNICH, MELBOURNE, DELHI

Editorial Assistant David Fentiman
Senior Editor Alastair Laing
Project Art Editor Kathryn Wilding
Senior Art Editor Sara Robin
US Editor Rebecca Warren
Managing Editor Dawn Henderson
Managing Art Editor Christine Keilty
Senior Jacket Creative Nicola Powling
Production Editor Siu Chan
Production Controller Claire Pearson
Creative Technical Support Sonia Charbonnier
Photographers Howard Shooter, Michael Hart

DK INDIA
Assistant Editor Ekta Sharma
Designer Prashant Kumar
Managing Editor Glenda Fernandes
Managing Art Editor Navidita Thapa
DTP Manager Sunil Sharma
DTP Operator Rajdeep Singh

First American Edition, 2012

First Published in the United States by
DK Publishing
375 Hudson Street
New York, New York 10014

11 12 13   10 9 8 7 6 5 4 3 2 1

001–180675–May/2012

Copyright © 2012 Dorling Kindersley Limited

Published in Great Britain by Dorling Kindersley Limited.

A catalog record for this book is available from the
Library of Congress.

US ISBN 978-0-7566-9267-4

DK books are available at special discounts when
purchased in bulk for sales promotions, premiums,
fund-raising, or educational use. For details, contact:
DK Publishing Special Markets, 375 Hudson Street,
New York, New York 10014 or SpecialSales@dk.com.

Color reproduction by Media Development Printing Ltd, UK

Printed and bound in Singapore by Tien Wah Press

Content previously published in
Illustrated Step-by-Step Baking

Discover more at www.dk.com

Contents

65 00033 7523

Chocoholic

RECIPE CHOOSERS

Triple-Layer Chocolate Cake
page 42

15 MINS   30–35 MINS

Chocolate and Hazelnut
Brownies page 182

25 MINS   12–15 MINS

Chocolate and Brazil
Nut Cake page 38

25 MINS   45–50 MINS

Prune Chocolate Dessert
Cake page 70

30 MINS   40–45 MINS

Chocolate Cake with
Buttercream page 40

30 MINS   20–25 MINS

Black Forest Gâteau
page 80

55 MINS   40 MINS

Pear and Chocolate Cake
page 43

15 MINS   30 MINS

Sour Cherry and Chocolate
Brownies page 186

15 MINS   20–25 MINS

Chocolate Fudge Cake
page 46

40 MINS 30 MINS

Baked Chocolate Mousse
page 48

20 MINS 1 HOUR

Chocolate Chestnut Roulade
page 76

50-55 MINS 5-7 MINS

Chocolate Cupcakes
page 100

20 MINS 20-25 MINS

Chocolate Amaretti Roulade
page 78

25-30 MINS 20 MINS

Chocolate Fudge Cake Balls
page 104

35 MINS 25 MINS

Chocolate Fondants
page 114

20 MINS 5-15 MINS

Chocolate Millefeuilles
page 92

2 HOURS 25-30 MINS

Get Fruity

Blueberry Upside Down Cake page 56

15 MINS 40 MINS

Cherry and Almond Cake page 57

20 MINS 1½–1¾ HOURS

Cherry Flapjacks page 180

15 MINS 25 MINS

Rich Fruit Cake page 66

25 MINS 2½ HOURS

Light Fruit Cake page 71

25 MINS 1¾ HOURS

Plum Pudding page 72

45 MINS 8–10 HOURS

Angel Food Cake page 20

30 MINS 35–45 MINS

Genoise Cake with Raspberries and Cream page 22

30 MINS 25–30 MINS

Lemon Polenta Cake page 36

30 MINS 50–60 MINS

Lemon and Blueberry Muffins
page 116

20–25 MINS   15–20 MINS

German Apple Cake
page 50

30 MINS   45–50 MINS

Bavarian Plum Cake
page 58

35–40 MINS   50–55 MINS

Banana Bread
page 60

20–25 MINS   35–40 MINS

Raspberry Cream Swiss Meringues page 134

10 MINS   1 HOUR

Strawberries and Cream Macarons page 158

30 MINS   18–20 MINS

Strawberry Shortcakes
page 125

15–20 MINS   12–15 MINS

Summer Fruit Millefeuilles
page 93

2 HOURS   25–30 MINS

Great for Kids

Vanilla Cream Cupcakes
page 96

20 MINS | 20–25 MINS

Fondant Fancies
page 102

20–25 MINS | 25 MINS

Gingerbread Men
page 148

20 MINS | 10–12 MINS

Whoopie Pies
page 108

40 MINS | 12 MINS

Strawberries and Cream Whoopie Pies page 113

40 MINS | 12 MINS

Apple Muffins
page 119

10 MINS | 20–25 MINS

Hazelnut and Raisin Oat Cookies page 140

20 MINS | 10–15 MINS

White Chocolate and Macadamia Nut Cookies page 143

25 MINS | 10–15 MINS

Spiced Carrot and Orange Cake page 33

20 MINS | 30 MINS

Chocolate Cupcakes
page 100

20 MINS | 20–25 MINS

Fast and Fabulous

Madeleines
page 120

15–20 MINS · 10 MINS

Welsh Cakes
page 126

20 MINS · 16–24 MINS

Swedish Spice Cookies
page 150

20 MINS · 10 MINS

Canestrelli
page 152

20 MINS · 15–20 MINS

Swiss Roll
page 24

20 MINS · 12–15 MINS

Pistachio and Cranberry Oat Cookies page 142

20 MINS · 10–15 MINS

Macaroons
page 154

10 MINS · 12–15 MINS

Cinnamon Stars
page 151

20 MINS · 12–15 MINS

Chocolate Fondants
page 114

20 MINS · 5–15 MINS

Chocolate Muffins
page 118

10 MINS · 15 MINS

everyday cakes

Victoria Sponge Cake

Probably the most iconic British cake, a good Victoria sponge should be well-risen, moist, and as light as air.

SERVES 6–8 | **30 MINS** | **20–25 MINS** | **4 WEEKS, UNFILLED**

Special equipment
2 x 8in (20cm) round cake pans

Ingredients
12 tbsp unsalted butter, softened, plus extra for greasing
¾ cup sugar
3 large eggs, at room temperature
1 tsp pure vanilla extract
1¼ cups all-purpose flour
1 tsp baking powder
½ tsp salt

For the filling
4 tbsp unsalted butter, softened
⅓ cup confectioner's sugar, plus more to serve
1 tsp pure vanilla extract
⅓ cup good-quality seedless raspberry jam

1 Preheat the oven to 350°F (180°C). Grease the cake pans and line with parchment paper.

2 Cream the butter and sugar with an electric mixer until fluffy, about 2 minutes.

3 Add the eggs one at a time, being sure to mix well between additions to prevent curdling.

4 Add the vanilla extract and beat briefly until it is well blended through the batter.

5 Beat the mixture for another 2 minutes until bubbles start to appear on the surface.

6 Remove the beaters, then sift the flour, baking powder, and salt into the bowl.

7 With a spoon, gently fold in the flour until just smooth. You can also mix in on low.

8 Divide the batter evenly between the pans, and smooth the tops with a palette knife.

9 Cook for 20 minutes or until golden brown and springy to the touch.

10 Test the sponges by inserting a skewer. If it comes out clean, the cakes are cooked.

11 Leave for a few minutes in the pans, then turn out on to a wire rack. Let cool completely.

12 For the filling, beat the butter, confectioner's sugar, and vanilla extract until smooth.

13 Spread the buttercream evenly onto the flat side of one sponge, using a palette knife.

14 Spread the raspberry jam in an even layer over the buttercream, right to the edges.

15 Top with the other sponge, flat sides together. Serve dusted with sifted confectioner's sugar.

STORE The filled cake will keep in an airtight container for 2 days. Unfilled, the sponges will keep for up to 3 days.

Victoria Sponge Cake variations

Coffee and Walnut Cake

A slice of coffee and walnut cake is the perfect accompaniment to morning coffee. Here the cake is made in smaller pans than the classic Victoria sponge to give it extra height and impact.

SERVES 8	20 MINS	20–25 MINS	8 WEEKS, UNFILLED

Special equipment
2 x 6¾in (17cm) round cake pans

Ingredients
12 tbsp unsalted butter, softened
1¼ cups all-purpose flour, plus extra for dusting
1 cup light brown sugar
3 large eggs, at room temperature
1 tsp pure vanilla extract
1 tsp baking powder
½ tsp salt
1 tbsp instant coffee mixed with 2 tbsp boiling water and cooled

For the frosting
7 tbsp unsalted butter, softened
1 cup confectioner's sugar
9 walnut halves

Method

1 Preheat the oven to 350°F (180°C). Grease the cake pans and dust with flour.

2 Cream the butter and sugar in an electric mixer or with an electric hand mixer until fluffy, about 2 minutes. Add the eggs one at a time, beating well between additions. Add the vanilla extract, and beat for another 2 minutes until bubbles appear on the surface. Sift in the flour, baking powder, and salt.

3 Mix in the flour on low until just smooth; try to keep the batter light. Fold in half the coffee mixture. Divide the batter evenly between the prepared pans, and smooth the tops with a palette knife.

4 Cook for 20–25 minutes or until golden and springy to the touch of a finger. Test the cakes by inserting a thin skewer. If it comes out clean, the cakes are cooked. Leave the cakes in the pans for a few minutes, then turn out on to a wire rack to cool completely.

5 To make the filling, beat the butter and confectioner's sugar together until smooth. Beat in the remaining coffee mixture. Spread half the buttercream evenly on to the flat side of one of the cakes. Top with the second cake, flat sides together, and spread with the remaining buttercream. Decorate with the walnut halves.

STORE The cake will keep in an airtight container in a cool place for 3 days.

Madeira Cake

In this simple cake, the flavors of lemon and butter shine through.

SERVES 8–10 | 20 MINS | 50–60 MINS | UP TO 8 WEEKS

Special equipment
8in (20cm) springform round cake pan

Ingredients
12 tbsp unsalted butter, softened
1½ cups all-purpose flour, plus extra for dusting
¾ cup sugar
3 large eggs, at room temperature
1½ tsp baking powder
½ tsp salt
finely grated zest of 1 lemon

Method
1 Preheat the oven to 350°F (180°C). Butter the cake pan and dust with flour.

2 Cream the butter and sugar in an electric mixer or with an electric hand mixer until fluffy, about 2 minutes. Add the eggs one at a time, mixing very well between additions.

3 Whisk for 2 minutes until bubbles appear on the surface. Sift in the flour, baking powder, and salt. Add the lemon zest. Mix in the flour mixture and zest on low until just smooth.

4 Spoon into the pan. Bake for 50–60 minutes or until a thin skewer comes out clean. Leave the cake in the pan for a couple of minutes, then turn out on to a wire rack to cool.

STORE The cake will keep in an airtight container for 3 days.

BAKER'S TIP
The secret to a good, light Victoria sponge-style cake is to ensure that as little air as possible is lost during the stage when the flour is added. For an even lighter finish, substitute margarine; the higher water content seems to bake air into the cake, though butter gives a richer flavor.

Marble Loaf Cake

For a twist on a classic sponge mixture, divide the batter in two and flavor half with cocoa before mixing them together for a wonderful marbled effect.

SERVES 8–10 | 25 MINS | 40–50 MINS | UP TO 8 WEEKS

Special equipment
9 x 5in (23 x 12cm) loaf pan

Ingredients
12 tbsp unsalted butter, softened, plus extra for greasing
1 cup all-purpose flour, plus more for dusting
¾ cup sugar
3 large eggs, at room temperature
1 tsp pure vanilla extract
1 tsp baking powder
½ tsp salt
¼ cup cocoa powder

Method
1 Preheat the oven to 350°F (180°C). Grease the loaf pan and dust with flour.

2 Cream the butter and sugar in an electric mixer or with an electric hand mixer until fluffy, about 2 minutes. Add the eggs one at a time, beating very well between additions. Add the vanilla extract, and beat for another 2 minutes until bubbles appear on the surface. Sift in the flour, baking powder, and salt. Mix on low just until smooth.

3 Divide the batter evenly between 2 bowls. Sift the cocoa powder into 1 of the bowls and fold in gently. Pour the vanilla cake batter into the loaf pan, then top with the chocolate batter. Using the end of a wooden spoon, a knife, or a skewer, swirl the 2 mixtures together, creating a marbled effect.

4 Cook for 45–50 minutes. Leave to cool slightly, then turn out on to a wire rack.

STORE The cake will keep in an airtight container for 3 days.

Angel Food Cake

This cake is as light as air. It contains no fat, so does not keep well, and is best enjoyed on the day of baking.

SERVES 8–12 · **30 MINS** · **35–45 MINS**

Special equipment
10in (25cm) tube pan with removable bottom
candy thermometer

Ingredients

For the cake
1¼ cups all-purpose flour
¾ cup confectioner's sugar

8 large egg whites
pinch of cream of tartar
1 cup sugar
few drops of almond or pure vanilla extract
fresh mixed berries, to serve

For the frosting
⅔ cup sugar
1 large egg white

Method

1 Preheat the oven to 350°F (180°C). Sift the flour and confectioner's sugar into a bowl.

2 Whisk the egg whites and cream of tartar until stiff, then whisk in the sugar, 1 tablespoon at a time. Gradually sift in the flour mixture, folding in with a metal spoon. Fold in the almond or pure vanilla extract.

3 Spoon the mixture gently into the tube pan, and level the surface with a palette knife. Place the pan on a baking sheet, and bake for 35-45 minutes, or until just firm to the touch.

4 Remove the cake from the oven, and invert the pan on to a wire rack. Leave the cake to cool completely, then run a knife around the edge and remove the bottom of the pan. Run the knife around the tube and the base to remove the cake from the pan.

5 To make the frosting, place the sugar in a saucepan with 4 tablespoons of water. Heat gently, stirring, until the sugar dissolves. Boil until the syrup reaches

soft-ball stage (238–245°F/114–118°C), or until a little of the syrup forms a soft ball when dropped into very cold water.

6 Meanwhile, whisk the egg white until stiff. As soon as the sugar syrup reaches the correct temperature, plunge the base of the pan into cold water to stop the syrup from getting any hotter, then pour slowly into the egg whites, still whisking, until the frosting forms stiff peaks.

7 Working quickly, because the frosting will set, spread it over the cake with a palette knife, swirling the surface to give texture. Serve with mixed berries.

STORE Angel food cake does not keep well, and the texture will change even on the second day, so avoid storing.

> **BAKER'S TIP**
> Sifting the flour twice produces a very light cake. For best results, try to lift the sieve high above the bowl, allowing the flour to come into contact with as much air as possible as it floats down. For an even lighter cake, sift the flour twice before sifting again into the egg mixture.

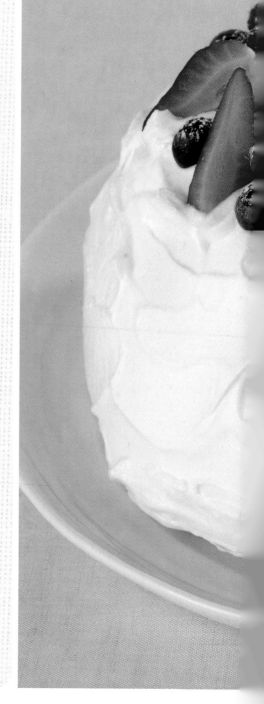

EVERYDAY CAKES

Genoise Cake with Raspberries and Cream

This delicate, whisked cake makes an impressive dessert, but is also ideal as the centerpiece for an afternoon picnic on a sunny summer's day.

SERVES 8–10 | **30 MINS** | **40 MINS** | **4 WEEKS, UNFILLED**

Special equipment
9in (20cm) springform cake pan

Ingredients

For the cake
3 tbsp unsalted butter, melted and cooled, plus extra for greasing

1 cup all-purpose flour, plus extra for dusting
4 large eggs
½ cup sugar
1 tsp pure vanilla extract
finely grated zest of 1 lemon

For the filling
2 cups heavy cream
11oz (325g) raspberries
1 tbsp confectioner's sugar, plus extra to serve

Method

1 Preheat the oven to 350°F (180°C). Grease the cake pan and dust with flour.

2 In an electric mixer with whisk attachment, or using a large bowl and a hand mixer, whisk together the eggs and sugar for at least 5 minutes, until they are thick, pale, and at least doubled in volume.

3 Sift the flour and carefully fold it into the mixture. Fold in the vanilla, lemon zest, and butter.

4 Put the batter into the cake pan and bake immediately for 40 minutes, or until the top is springy and a skewer inserted into the middle of the cake comes out clean.

5 Leave the cake to cool in the pan for a few minutes, then turn out and leave to cool completely on a wire rack.

6 When the cake is cold, cut it very carefully horizontally into three equal pieces, using a serrated bread knife.

7 In a large bowl, whip the cream until stiff. Crush the raspberries lightly with the confectioner's sugar and fold into the cream, leaving behind any juice so that the cream is not too wet.

8 Spread half the cream and raspberry mixture onto one piece of the cake, and top with a second piece. Spread the remaining cream mixture on to the second layer of cake and top with the final layer. Dust the cake with confectioner's sugar and serve immediately.

PREPARE AHEAD The cake will keep, unfilled, in an airtight container for one day.

BAKER'S TIP
This is a classic Italian cake that uses very little fat, and only a little melted butter, for flavor. These cakes are infinitely adaptable, and can be filled with anything you like, but should ideally be eaten within 24 hours of baking, because the lack of fat means they do not store as well as other cakes.

Swiss Roll

There is a trick to rolling up a Swiss roll—follow these simple steps and yours will come out perfectly every time.

SERVES 8–10	20 MINS	12–15 MINS	8 WEEKS, UNFILLED

Special equipment
17 x 11in (43 x 28cm) jelly roll pan

Ingredients
3 large eggs
½ cup sugar, plus more to sprinkle
1 tsp pure vanilla extract
pinch of salt
½ cup all-purpose flour
½ tsp baking powder
6 tbsp strawberry jam, raspberry
   jam, or chocolate-hazelnut spread

1 Preheat the oven to 400°F (200°C). Line the jelly roll pan with parchment paper.

2 Set a bowl over a pan of simmering water; the base of the bowl shouldn't touch the water.

3 Whisk the eggs, sugar, vanilla, and salt with a hand mixer or whisk for 5 minutes, until thick.

4 Test the mixture is ready: drips from the beaters should stay formed for a few seconds.

5 Remove the bowl from the pan. Place it on a work surface. Whisk for 1–2 minutes until cool.

6 Sift in the flour, baking powder, and salt over the egg mixture and fold in very gently.

7 Pour onto the pan and level into the corners, smoothing the top with a palette knife.

8 Bake for 10–12 minutes, until firm and springy to the touch of a finger.

9 Check that the cake has shrunk away from the sides of the pan; this shows it is ready.

10 Sprinkle a large sheet of parchment paper evenly with a thin layer of sugar.

11 Carefully turn the Swiss roll out of its pan onto the sugar, so it lies upside down.

12 Leave to cool for 5 minutes, then carefully peel the parchment from the cake.

13 If the jam is too thick to spread, warm it gently in a small pan.

14 Spread the jam evenly over the top of the cake, being sure to reach all the edges.

15 Make an indent with the back of a knife along one short side, ¾in (2cm) from the edge.

16 With the indented side facing you, carefully start to roll the cake up, being gentle but firm.

17 Use the parchment paper to keep the cake tightly rolled and in shape. Leave to cool.

18 Peel off the parchment and place the cake, seam-side down, on a serving plate. Sprinkle with sugar. **STORE** It will keep in an airtight container for 2 days.

Swiss Roll variations

Orange and Pistachio Swiss Roll

Using the delicate flavors of pistachio nuts and orange flower water gives this classic recipe a slightly more modern twist. It is easily portioned and makes an ideal dessert for large parties and buffets.

SERVES 8 | **20 MINS** | **15 MINS** | **8 WEEKS, UNFILLED**

Special equipment
17 x 11in (43 x 28cm) jelly roll pan

Ingredients
½ cup sugar, plus more to sprinkle
3 large eggs
½ cup all-purpose flour
½ tsp baking powder
pinch of salt
finely grated zest of 2 oranges and 3 tbsp juice
2 tsp orange flower water (optional)
confectioner's sugar, to dust
2½ oz (75g) unsalted shelled pistachio nuts
¾ cup heavy cream

Method
1 Preheat the oven to 400°F (200°C). Line the pan with parchment. Combine sugar and eggs in a heatproof bowl set over simmering water; the base should not touch the water.

2 Whisk the mixture with an electric hand mixer or balloon whisk for 5 minutes, or until thick and creamy. Drips from the beaters should briefly sit on the surface.

3 Remove the bowl from the pan. Whisk for 1-2 minutes until cool. Sift in the flour, baking powder, and salt over the egg mixture, and add half the zest and 1 tablespoon orange juice. Fold together.

4 Pour onto the pan and level into corners, smoothing with a palette knife. Bake for 10-12 minutes, or until firm to the touch and the cake has shrunk away from the sides.

5 Sprinkle a large sheet of parchment paper evenly with sugar. Carefully turn the cake onto the sugar. Leave to cool for 5 minutes, then carefully peel the parchment from the cake. Sprinkle with orange water.

6 Make an indent with the back of a knife along one short side, about ¾in (2cm) from the edge. With this side facing you, carefully roll the cake up, using the parchment to keep the cake in shape. Leave to cool.

7 For the filling, chop the nuts and set aside. Whip the cream, and fold in the nuts, remaining zest, and juice. Unroll the cake and spread with cream. Discard the parchment and carefully place the cake, seam-side down, on a serving plate or cake stand, and dust with confectioner's sugar. Serve immediately.

> **BAKER'S TIP**
> If a recipe requires a Swiss roll to be completely cool before filling, the cake will need to be rolled into shape while still warm, and then unrolled. Roll the cake around a fresh sheet of parchment paper. This will prevent the layers from sticking and allow the cake to be rolled tightly for a neat shape, and easily unrolled.

Spanish Rolled Sponge Cake

In this sophisticated Spanish take on Swiss roll, a tangy lemon sponge is rolled around a smooth filling of chocolate-rum ganache, forming a pretty spiral for slicing. Impressive as a dinner party dessert. ▶

SERVES 8–10 | **40–45 MINS** | **7–9 MINS** | **8 WEEKS, UNFILLED**

Chilling time
6 hours

Ingredients
butter, for greasing
⅔ cup sugar
5 eggs, separated
finely grated zest of 2 lemons
⅓ cup all-purpose flour, sifted
pinch of salt
½ cup confectioner's sugar
1 tsp ground cinnamon
candied lemon zest, to serve (optional)

For the ganache
4½ oz (125g) dark chocolate, coarsely chopped
⅔ cup heavy cream
½ tsp ground cinnamon
1½ tbsp dark rum

Method
1 Preheat the oven to 425°F (220°C). Grease and line a baking sheet with parchment paper. Mix ½ cup sugar with the egg yolks and zest. With an electric mixer, beat for 3–5 minutes until thick. In a metal bowl, whisk the egg whites until stiff. Sprinkle in the remaining sugar and whisk until glossy. Add the salt to the yolk mix, then sift and fold in the flour and the egg whites.

2 Pour the mixture on to the prepared baking sheet and spread it almost to the edges. Bake near the bottom of the oven for 7–9 minutes, until firm and golden brown. Remove the cake from the oven, remove the parchment, and roll up. Let cool.

3 For the ganache, put the chocolate in a large bowl. Heat the cream with the cinnamon in a small saucepan until almost boiling. Add to the chocolate and stir until melted. Let cool and add the rum. Beat the ganache with an electric whisk for 5–10 minutes, until thick and fluffy.

4 Mix half the confectioner's sugar with cinnamon in a small sieve. Sprinkle the mixture evenly over a large sheet of parchment paper. Place the cake on the sugared paper and gently unroll it. Spread the ganache evenly over the cake. Carefully roll up the filled cake as before and chill for about 6 hours, or until the filling is firm. Unwrap the cake, trim each end, sift over the remaining confectioner's sugar, and scatter with candied lemon zest (if using).

EVERYDAY CAKES

Ginger Cake

Deeply flavored with preserved ginger, this rich and moist ginger cake is a firm favorite, and keeps well for up to a week—should it last that long!

| SERVES 12 | 20 MINS | 35–45 MINS | UP TO 8 WEEKS |

Special equipment
8in (20cm) square cake pan

Ingredients
8 tbsp unsalted butter, softened,
  plus extra for greasing
1 cup corn syrup
½ cup dark brown sugar
¾ cup milk
4 tbsp syrup from preserved ginger jar
finely grated zest of 1 orange
1½ cups all-purpose flour
1 tsp baking powder
¼ tsp salt
1 tsp baking soda
1 tsp pumpkin pie spice
1 tsp cinnamon
2 tsp ground ginger
4 pieces of preserved ginger, finely chopped
  and tossed in 1 tbsp all-purpose flour
1 large egg, lightly beaten

Method

1 Preheat the oven to 340°F (170°C). Grease the cake pan and line the base with parchment paper.

2 In a saucepan, gently heat the corn syrup, sugar, butter, milk, and ginger syrup until the butter has melted. Add the orange zest and leave to cool for 5 minutes.

3 In a large mixing bowl, sift together the flour, baking powder, salt, baking soda, and ground spices. Pour the warm liquid ingredients into the dry ingredients and beat them well, using a balloon whisk. Stir in the preserved ginger and egg.

4 Pour the batter into the pan and cook for 35–45 minutes, until a skewer inserted into the middle of the cake comes out clean. Leave to cool in the pan for at least 1 hour before turning out to cool on a wire rack. Remove the parchment paper before serving.

STORE This cake is very moist and keeps well in an airtight container for up to 1 week.

BAKER'S TIP
The use of corn syrup and dark brown sugar here gives a dense, moist cake that keeps very well. If the cake is beginning to get a little dry with age, try slicing it and spreading with butter as a breakfast snack, or even turning it into a rich bread pudding.

Carrot Cake

For a more luxurious cake, double the frosting, slice the cake in two, and fill the middle as well.

SERVES 8–10

20 MINS

45 MINS

UP TO 8 WEEKS

Special equipment
9in (22cm) round springform cake pan
zester

Ingredients
1 cup (4oz) walnuts
¾ cup sunflower or vegetable oil, plus extra for greasing
3 large eggs
1 tsp pure vanilla extract
1¼ cup light brown sugar
2 cups packed, coarsely grated carrots (about 3 small carrots)
⅔ cup (3oz) golden raisins

1½ cups all-purpose flour, plus extra for dusting
½ cup whole wheat flour
2 tsp baking powder
½ tsp salt
1 tsp cinnamon
1 tsp ground ginger
about ¼ tsp finely grated nutmeg
finely grated zest of 1 orange

For the cream cheese frosting
4 tbsp unsalted butter, softened
⅓ cup cream cheese, room temp
½ tsp pure vanilla extract
1½ cups confectioner's sugar
finely grated zest of ½ an orange

1 Preheat the oven to 350°F (180°C). Bake the walnuts for 5 minutes, until lightly browned.

2 Put the nuts into a clean kitchen towel and rub them to remove excess skin.

3 Pour the oil and eggs into a large bowl, add the vanilla, and pour in the sugar.

4 Using an electric hand mixer, beat the oil mixture until it appears lighter and thickened.

5 Squeeze the grated carrot very well in a clean kitchen towel to remove excess liquid.

6 Gently fold the carrot into the cake batter, ensuring it is evenly blended throughout.

7 By now, the walnuts should be cool. Coarsely chop them, leaving some large pieces.

8 Add the walnuts to the mixture, along with the raisins, and gently fold them in.

9 Sift over the two types of flour and baking powder, then add in any bran left in the sieve.

10 Add the salt, spices, and orange zest, and fold all the ingredients together to combine.

11 Oil the base and sides of the cake pan and dust with flour. Pour the cake batter into pan.

12 Bake for 45 minutes. Test by inserting a skewer into the cake; it should come out clean.

13 If not, bake for a few more minutes and test again. Transfer to a wire rack to cool.

14 Combine the butter, cream cheese, vanilla, and confectioner's sugar, then grate in the zest.

15 Using an electric mixer, cream together ingredients until smooth, paler, and fluffy.

16 Using a palette knife, spread the frosting over the cake. Make swirls for texture.

17 For additional decoration, zest the remaining orange using a zester tool.

18 Carefully place the finished cake on a serving plate or cake stand. Decorate the cake with the strands of orange zest. **STORE** The cake will keep in an airtight container for 3 days.

Carrot Cake variations

Zucchini Cake

This intriguing alternative to carrot cake is a true favorite.

| SERVES 8–10 | 20 MINS | 45 MINS | UP TO 2 MONTHS |

Special equipment
9in (22cm) round springform cake pan

Ingredients
1 cup sunflower oil, plus extra for greasing
1½ cups all-purpose flour, plus more for dusting
¾ cup (4oz) hazelnuts
3 large eggs
1 tsp pure vanilla extract
1 cup sugar
1½ cups coarsely grated zucchini (1 small)
½ cup whole wheat flour
2 tsp baking powder
1 tsp cinnamon
½ tsp salt
finely grated zest of 1 lemon

Method

1 Preheat the oven to 350°F (180°C). Oil the base and sides of the pan and dust with flour. Spread hazelnuts on a baking sheet and cook for 5 minutes, until lightly browned. Put the nuts on a clean kitchen towel and rub them to get rid of excess skin. Coarsely chop and set aside.

2 Pour the oil and eggs into a bowl, add the vanilla, and pour in the sugar. Mix the oil mixture until lighter and thickened. Squeeze moisture from the zucchini and fold in with the nuts. Sift over the flour, add in any bran left in the sieve. Add the salt, cinnamon, and lemon zest, and fold.

3 Pour the batter into the pan. Bake for 45 minutes, or until springy to the touch. Turn out to cool completely on a wire rack.

STORE The cake will keep in an airtight container for 3 days.

BAKER'S TIP
Don't be put off by the unusual inclusion of zucchini. Zucchini are less sweet than carrots, but add moisture and a fresh flavor. The lack of frosting makes this cake healthier, too.

Quick Carrot Cake

Carrot cakes are perfect for novice bakers because they do not require lengthy whisking or delicate folding. This popular variation is very moist and will disappear fast.

SERVES 8 · **15 MINS** · **20–25 MINS** · **UP TO 8 WEEKS**

Special equipment
8in (20cm) round cake pan

Ingredients

For the cake
¾ cup vegetable oil, plus some extra
  for greasing
1 cup all-purpose flour, plus some extra
  for dusting
½ tsp ground allspice
1 tsp baking powder
½ tsp ground ginger
¼ tsp salt
2 carrots (about 1 heaping cup), coarsely grated
½ cup light brown sugar
⅓ cup (2oz) golden raisins
2 eggs, beaten
1 tbsp fresh orange juice

For the frosting
½ cup cream cheese, at room temperature
2 tbsp unsalted butter, softened
⅔ cup confectioner's sugar
2 tbsp fresh orange juice
lemon zest, to decorate

Method
1 Preheat the oven to 375°F (190°C). Grease the cake pan and dust with flour. Sift the flour, allspice, baking powder, ginger, and salt into a large bowl. Add the carrots, sugar, and golden raisins, then stir to mix.

2 Add the eggs, orange juice, and the oil. Stir together until well blended.

3 Pour in the cake mixture, and level the surface using a palette knife. Bake for 20 minutes, or until a skewer inserted into the center comes out clean. Let stand in the pan for 10 minutes, to cool.

4 Run a knife around the sides, invert onto a wire rack, and leave to cool completely.

5 Meanwhile, beat the cream cheese with the rest of the orange juice and the confectioner's sugar. Spread the frosting over the top of the cake and decorate with lemon zest.

STORE The cake will keep in an airtight container for 3 days.

Spiced Carrot and Orange Cake

A fabulous cake for winter, with hints of warming spice and zesty orange. Baking it in a square pan allows the cake to be cut into bite-sized pieces, perfect for a party. **PICTURED OVERLEAF**

MAKES 16 SQUARES · **20 MINS** · **30 MINS** · **UP TO 8 WEEKS**

Special equipment
8in (20cm) square cake pan

Ingredients

For the cake
⅔ cup sunflower oil or light olive oil, plus extra
  for greasing
1 ½ cups all-purpose flour, plus extra for dusting
1 tsp ground cinnamon
1 tsp pumpkin pie spice
1 ½ tsp baking soda
½ tsp salt
½ cup brown sugar
2 large eggs
⅓ cup corn syrup
1 packed cup coarsely grated carrots (2 carrots)
finely grated zest of 1 orange

For the frosting
½ cup confectioner's sugar
⅓ cup cream cheese, at room temperature
1–2 tbsp orange juice
finely grated zest of 1 orange, plus extra
  to decorate (optional)
finely grated zest of 1 orange, plus extra
  to decorate (optional)

Method
1 Preheat the oven to 350°F (180°C). Grease the cake pan and dust with flour. In a large bowl, mix together the flour, spices, baking soda, salt, and sugar.

2 In another bowl, mix the oil, eggs, and syrup, then combine with the dry ingredients. Stir in the carrot and zest, transfer to the pan, and level the top.

3 Bake for 30 minutes, or until firm to the touch. Leave in the pan for a few minutes, then turn out to cool completely on a wire rack.

4 For the frosting, sift the confectioner's sugar into a bowl, add the cream cheese, orange juice, and orange zest, and beat with an electric hand mixer until thick and spreadable. Spread the frosting over the cake. Decorate with extra orange zest (if using), and cut into squares.

STORE The cake will keep in an airtight container for 3 days.

Lemon Polenta Cake

One of the few wheat-free cakes that work just as well as those made from wheat flour.

SERVES 6–8

30 MINS

50–60 MINS

UP TO 8 WEEKS

Special equipment
9in (22cm) round springform pan

Ingredients
12 tbsp unsalted butter, softened, plus extra for greasing
7oz (200g) sugar
3 large eggs
½ cup polenta or coarse-ground cornmeal
1⅓ cups (6oz) ground almonds
finely grated zest and juice of 2 lemons
1 tsp gluten-free baking powder

1 Preheat the oven to 325°F (160°C). Grease the pan and line the base with parchment paper.

2 By hand, or in an electric mixer, cream the butter and 6oz (175g) of the sugar until fluffy.

3 Whisk the eggs and gradually beat them into the creamed mixture.

4 Fold in the polenta and almonds, or gently pulse-blend in a processor until well blended.

5 Finally mix in the lemon zest and baking powder well. The batter will seem stiff.

6 Scrape the mixture into the prepared pan and smooth the surface with a palette knife.

7 Bake the cake for 50–60 minutes, until springy to the touch. It will not rise much.

8 Check that the cake is cooked by inserting a skewer. The skewer should emerge clean.

9 Leave the cake in the pan for a few minutes, until cool enough to handle.

10 Meanwhile, put the lemon juice and the remaining sugar in a small saucepan.

11 Heat the juice over medium heat until the sugar has completely dissolved.

12 Turn the cake out on to a wire rack, baked side up, peeling off the parchment paper.

13 Using a thin skewer or toothpick, poke holes in the top of the cake while still warm.

14 Pour the hot lemon syrup a little at a time over the surface of the cake.

15 Only once the syrup has soaked into the cake, pour more on, until it is all used up.

16 Once cooled, serve the cake at room temperature on its own or with heavy cream or whipped cream. **STORE** The cake will keep in an airtight container for 3 days.

Wheat-free Cake variations

Chocolate and Brazil Nut Cake

This unusual wheat-free cake uses Brazil nuts instead of the typical almond and chocolate combination, to give a moist, rich finish to the cake.

SERVES 6–8 | **25 MINS** | **45–50 MINS** | **UP TO 4 WEEKS**

Special equipment
8in (20cm) round springform cake pan
food processor

Ingredients
5 tbsp unsalted butter, cubed,
  plus extra for greasing
3½oz (100g) good-quality dark chocolate,
  chopped
5½oz (150g) Brazil nuts
½ cup sugar
4 large eggs, separated
cocoa powder or confectioner's sugar, to serve

Method
1 Preheat the oven to 350°F (180°C). Grease the cake pan and line the base with parchment paper. Melt the chocolate in a bowl over a little simmering water (don't let the base of the bowl touch the water).

2 In a food processor, grind the Brazil nuts and sugar as finely as possible. Add the butter and pulse just until blended in. Continue to blend while adding the egg yolks one at a time. Add the melted chocolate and blend in thoroughly.

3 In a separate bowl, whisk the egg whites to stiff peaks. Turn the chocolate mixture into a large bowl and beat in a few tablespoons of the egg whites to loosen the mixture. Now carefully fold in the remaining egg whites.

4 Scrape into the pan and bake for 45–50 minutes, until the surface is springy and a skewer inserted into the middle of the cake comes out clean. Allow to cool in the pan for a few minutes, then turn out to cool completely on a wire rack. Remove the parchment paper. Sift over the cocoa powder or confectioner's sugar and serve with whipped cream.

STORE The cake will keep in an airtight container for 3 days.

> ### BAKER'S TIP
> This cake is a delicious dessert with thick cream. Be careful to pulse the butter into the nut and sugar mixture in short bursts—prolonged blending will release the oils in the nuts and give the finished cake an oily flavor.

Torta margherita

This Italian classic is made with potato flour and is as light as air.

SERVES 6–8 | **20 MINS** | **25–30 MINS** | **UP TO 8 WEEKS**

Special equipment
8in (20cm) round springform cake pan

Ingredients
2 tbsp unsalted butter, melted and cooled, plus
  extra for greasing
2 large eggs, plus 1 egg yolk
½ cup sugar
½ tsp pure vanilla extract
½ cup potato flour, sifted
½ tsp baking powder
finely grated zest of ½ lemon
confectioner's sugar, for dusting

Method
1 Preheat the oven to 350°F (180°C). Grease the pan and line the base with parchment paper.

2 In a large bowl, using an electric hand mixer, or an electric mixer with a whisk attachment, whisk the eggs, egg yolk, sugar, and vanilla extract together for at least 5 minutes, until thick, pale, and at least doubled in size. Gently fold in the potato flour, baking powder, and lemon zest, then fold in the butter.

3 Scrape the batter into the prepared pan and bake for 25–30 minutes, until the surface is golden brown and springy to the touch, and a skewer inserted into the middle comes out clean.

4 Leave the cake to cool for 10 minutes in its pan, then turn out to cool completely on a wire rack. Remove the parchment. Dust with confectioner's sugar to serve.

STORE The torta will keep in an airtight container for 2 days.

Castagnaccio

A traditional cake with a dense, moist texture.

SERVES 6–8   **25 MINS**   **50–60 MINS**

Special equipment
8in (20cm) round springform cake pan

Ingredients
1 tbsp olive oil, plus extra for greasing
⅓ cup (2oz) raisins
¼ cup (scant 1oz) sliced almonds
¼ cup (scant 1oz) pine nuts
3 cups chestnut flour
2 tbsp sugar
pinch of salt
1¾ cup milk or water
1 tbsp finely chopped rosemary leaves
zest of 1 orange

Method
1 Preheat the oven to 350°F (180°C). Grease the cake pan and line the base with parchment paper. Cover the raisins in warm water and leave for 5 minutes to plump them up. Drain.

2 Put the almonds and pine nuts on a baking sheet and toast gently for 5–10 minutes, until lightly browned. Sift the chestnut flour into a large mixing bowl. Add the sugar and salt.

3 Using a balloon whisk, gradually whisk in the milk or water to produce a thick, smooth batter. Whisk in the olive oil and pour the batter into the pan. Scatter over the raisins, rosemary, zest, and nuts.

4 Bake at the center of the oven for 50–60 minutes until the surface is dry and cracked and the edges slightly browned. The cake will not really rise. Leave in the pan for 10 minutes, then carefully turn it out and leave it to cool completely on a wire rack. Remove the parchment paper.

STORE The Castagnaccio will keep in an airtight container for 3 days.

NOTE Chestnut flour is available from Italian delicatessens.

Chocolate Cake with Buttercream

Everyone loves a classic chocolate cake, and in this version the yogurt in the mix makes it extra moist.

SERVES 6-8	30 MINS	20-25 MINS	8 WEEKS, UNFILLED

Special equipment
2 x 6¾in (17cm) round cake pans

Ingredients
14 tbsp unsalted butter, softened,
   plus extra for greasing
½ cup cocoa powder, plus extra for
   dusting
¾ cup light brown sugar
3 large eggs
⅔ cup all-purpose flour
1 tsp baking powder
¼ tsp salt
¼ cup Greek, or thick plain yogurt

For the chocolate buttercream
4 tbsp unsalted butter, softened
⅔ cup confectioner's sugar, sifted,
   plus extra to serve
¼ cup cocoa powder
a little milk, if necessary

1 Preheat the oven to 350°F (180°C). Grease the pans with butter and dust with cocoa powder.

2 Place the butter and sugar into a large bowl, or in the bowl of an electric mixer.

3 With an electric hand mixer, or in the electric mixer, cream the mixture until light and fluffy.

4 Beat in the eggs one at a time, beating well after each addition, until well mixed.

5 In a separate bowl, sift together the flour, cocoa powder, baking powder, and salt.

6 Fold the flour mixture into the cake batter until well blended, trying to keep volume.

7 Gently fold through the thick yogurt. This will help to make the cake moist.

8 Divide the mixture between the 2 cake pans, smoothing the surfaces with a palette knife.

9 Bake in the middle of the oven for 20-25 minutes until risen and springy to the touch.

10 Test each cake by inserting a skewer into the middle; it should come out clean.

11 Leave the cakes in their pans for a few minutes then turn out on to a wire rack to cool.

12 For the buttercream, put butter, sugar, and cocoa powder into a large bowl.

13 With an electric hand mixer, blend the mixture for 5 minutes, or until light and fluffy.

14 If the cream is stiff, add milk, 1 teaspoon at a time, until it reaches a spreading consistency.

15 Spread the flat base of one sponge with the buttercream, then top with the other sponge.

16 Place on a serving plate and sift confectioner's sugar evenly over the cake.
STORE The cake will keep in an airtight container for 2 days.

Chocolate Cake variations

Triple-Layer Chocolate Cake

Moist cake, fluffy vanilla cream, and smooth chocolate icing—everything a chocolate and cake lover could wish for.

SERVES 12 | 15 MINS | 30–35 MINS

Special equipment
3 x 8in (20cm) round cake pans

Ingredients
2⅓ cups all-purpose flour
4 tbsp cocoa powder
1 heaped tsp baking powder
1 stick unsalted butter, softened, plus 4 tbsp
  and extra for greasing
½ cup sugar, plus 1 tbsp
5 large eggs
1 tsp vanilla extract, plus a few drops
4 tbsp milk
6oz (175g) semisweet chocolate
2 cups heavy cream

Method

1 Preheat the oven to 350°F (180°C). Grease the cake pans and line the bases with parchment paper. Sift the flour, cocoa, and baking powder together into a bowl. Cream the sugar and all but 2 tablespoons of the butter in a separate bowl with an electric mixer until pale and fluffy.

2 Add the sifted flour, eggs, vanilla, and milk, then beat for 1 minute, until the mixture is uniform and fluffy. Divide evenly between the 3 cake pans and level the tops. Bake in the oven for 30–35 minutes. Leave the cakes to cool in the pans for 5 minutes, then turn out on to a wire rack, and leave until cold.

3 Break off 2oz (50g) of the chocolate and push a vegetable peeler across the surface to form curls. Set aside in a cool place.

4 Measure ⅔ cup of the cream into a heatproof bowl. Break the remaining chocolate into squares and add to the bowl. Place over a pan of gently simmering water, making sure the base of the bowl doesn't touch the water, and stir until the chocolate melts and a smooth shiny icing forms. Remove from the heat, stir in 2 tablespoons butter, and leave to cool.

5 Pour the remaining cream into a bowl, add 1 tablespoon sugar, a few drops of vanilla, and whisk until soft peaks form. Divide the cream between 2 of the cakes, stack them on top of each other, then cover with the third cake. Spoon the cooled icing over the top, letting it run down the sides. Sprinkle with the chocolate curls, and serve.

Fudge-Frosted Chocolate Cake

Always a crowd-pleaser, this cake is a must for your repertoire.

SERVES 8–12 | 20 MINS | 40 MINS | UP TO 8 WEEKS

Special equipment
2 x 8in (20cm) round cake pans

Ingredients
16 tbsp unsalted butter, plus extra for greasing
1½ cups all-purpose flour
¼ cups cocoa powder, plus extra for dusting
4 large eggs
1 cup sugar
1 tsp pure vanilla extract
1 tsp baking powder

For the chocolate fudge frosting
⅓ cup cocoa powder
1¼ cups confectioner's sugar
3 tbsp unsalted butter, melted
3 tbsp milk, plus extra to thin the mixture

Method

1 Preheat the oven to 350°F (180°C). Grease the pans, then dust with flour and cocoa powder. Sift the flour and cocoa powder into a bowl, and add all the other cake ingredients. Whisk together with an electric hand mixer for a few minutes until well combined. Whisk in 2 tablespoons of warm water so the mixture is soft. Divide evenly between the pans, and smooth the tops.

2 Bake for 35–40 minutes or until risen and firm to the touch. Leave to cool in the pans for a few minutes before turning out onto wire racks to cool completely.

3 For the frosting, sift the cocoa powder and sugar into a bowl, add the butter and milk, and mix with an electric hand mixer until smooth and well combined. Add a little extra milk if the mixture is too thick; you need to be able to spread it easily. Spread over the tops of the cooled cakes, then sandwich together.

STORE The cake will keep for 2 days in an airtight container.

Pear and Chocolate Cake

This rich, luscious cake is a good choice when you want to impress.

SERVES 6–8   **15 MINS**   **30 MINS**

Special equipment
8in (20cm) round springform cake pan

Ingredients
9 tbsp unsalted butter, plus extra for greasing
½ cup cocoa powder, sifted, plus more
  for dusting
2 cups all-purpose flour, sifted
2 tsp baking powder
1 tsp salt
¾ cup sugar
4 large eggs, lightly beaten
2oz (50g) dark chocolate, chopped
  (see Baker's Tip)
2 pears, peeled, cored, and chopped
⅔ cup milk
confectioner's sugar, for dusting

Method
1 Preheat the oven to 350°F (180°C). Grease the pan with butter and dust with cocoa powder. Sift flour, cocoa powder, baking powder, and salt into a medium bowl.

2 Cream the butter with the sugar using a wooden spoon or an electric hand mixer until pale and creamy. Beat in the eggs. Then add the flour mixture gradually, adding a little of the milk each time until all of it is combined. Fold in the chopped chocolate and pears.

3 Pour the cake mixture into the prepared pan, put it in the oven, and bake for 30-45 minutes, or until firm and springy to the touch. Allow to cool in the pan for 15 minutes, then remove from the pan, and transfer the cake to a wire rack to cool completely. Sift over confectioner's sugar before serving.

STORE The cake will keep in an airtight container for 2 days.

Devil's Food Cake

This American classic uses the flavor of coffee to enhance the richness of the chocolate, adding a wonderful depth to the finished cake.

| SERVES 8–10 | 30 MINS | 30–35 MINS | 8 WEEKS, UNFILLED |

Special equipment
2 x 8in (20cm) cake pans

Ingredients
7 tbsp unsalted butter, softened, plus extra
 for greasing
⅔ cup cocoa powder, plus more for dusting
1¼ cups sugar
2 large eggs, at room temperature

1½ cups all-purpose flour
1½ tsp baking powder
½ tsp salt
½ cup strong cold coffee
½ cup milk
1 tsp pure vanilla extract

For the frosting
1 stick unsalted butter, diced
¼ cup cocoa powder
¾ cup confectioner's sugar
2–3 tbsp milk
chocolate, for the shavings

Method

1 Preheat the oven to 350°F (180°C). Grease the cake pans and dust them with cocoa powder. By hand, or in an electric mixer, cream together the butter and sugar until light and fluffy.

2 Beat in the eggs one at a time, beating well after each addition, until well mixed. In a separate bowl, sift together the flour, cocoa powder, baking powder, and salt. In another bowl, mix together the cooled coffee, milk, and vanilla extract.

3 Next, beat alternate spoonfuls of the dry and liquid ingredients into the cake batter. Once the mixture is well blended, divide it between the pans.

4 Bake for 30–35 minutes, until the cake is springy to the touch and a skewer inserted into the middle comes out clean. Leave to cool in the pans for a few minutes, then turn out to cool completely on a wire rack.

5 For the frosting, melt the butter in a saucepan over low heat. Add the cocoa powder and continue to cook for a minute or two, stirring frequently. Allow the mixture to cool slightly.

6 Sift in the confectioner's sugar, beating thoroughly to combine. Blend, adding the milk 1 tablespoon at a time, until smooth and glossy. Allow to cool (it will thicken), then use half to sandwich the cakes together and the remainder to decorate the top and sides of the cake. Finally, use a vegetable peeler to create chocolate shavings and scatter them evenly over the top of the cake.

STORE This cake will keep in an airtight container in a cool place for 5 days.

BAKER'S TIP

Don't be put off by the inclusion of coffee in this recipe. Even if you don't normally like coffee-flavored cakes, use it here, as its inclusion gives a deep, dark fudgy texture to the chocolate cake, and also subtly enhances the chocolate flavor, rather than an overt coffee taste.

Chocolate Fudge Cake

Everyone should have a chocolate fudge cake recipe, and this one is a winner. The oil and syrup keep it moist, and the frosting is a classic.

| SERVES 6–8 | 40 MINS | 30 MINS | 8 WEEKS, UNFILLED |

Special equipment
2 x 8in (20cm) cake pans

Ingredients
⅔ cup sunflower oil, plus extra for greasing
¼ cup cocoa powder, plus extra for dusting
1¼ cups all-purpose flour
1 tsp baking powder
½ tsp salt
¾ cup light brown sugar
3 tbsp corn syrup
2 large eggs, at room temperature
⅔ cup milk

For the frosting
8 tbsp unsalted butter, at room temperature
¼ cup cocoa powder
¾ cup confectioner's sugar
2 tbsp milk, if necessary

Method

1 Preheat the oven to 350°F (180°C). Grease the pans and dust with cocoa powder. In a large bowl, sift together the flour, cocoa, baking powder, and salt. Mix in the sugar.

2 Gently heat the corn syrup until runny and leave to cool. In a separate bowl, using an electric hand mixer or balloon whisk, beat together the eggs, sunflower oil, and milk.

3 Whisk the egg mixture into the flour mixture until well combined. Gently add the syrup and divide the batter between the pans.

4 Bake the cakes in the middle of the oven for about 30 minutes, until springy to the touch, and a skewer inserted into the middle comes out clean. Leave to cool in the pans for a few minutes, then turn out to cool completely on a wire rack.

5 To make the frosting, melt the butter over low heat. Stir in the cocoa powder and cook gently for a minute or two, then leave to cool. Sift the confectioner's sugar into a bowl.

6 Pour the cooled melted butter and cocoa into the confectioner's sugar and beat to combine. If the mixture seems dry add the milk, 1 tablespoon at a time, until you have a smooth, glossy frosting. Leave to cool for up to 30 minutes. It will thicken as it cools.

7 When thick, use half the frosting to fill the cake and the other half to top it.

STORE This cake will keep in an airtight container for 3 days.

BAKER'S TIP
The frosting used here is a real staple in my kitchen, and can be used to finish so many chocolate recipes. Leftovers that are slightly old can be heated for 30 seconds in a microwave, where the frosting will melt into a rich sauce, and can be served with vanilla ice cream for a delicious, quick dessert.

Baked Chocolate Mousse

Classic, but very easy to make, even for a novice. Slice the moist, fragile mousse with a sharp knife dipped in hot water, and wipe between cuts.

SERVES **20** **1**
8–12 **MINS** **HOUR**

Special equipment
9in (23cm) round springform cake pan

Ingredients
18 tbsp unsalted butter, cubed
12oz (350g) dark chocolate, broken into pieces
1½ cups light brown sugar
5 large eggs, at room temperature, separated
pinch of salt
cocoa powder or confectioner's sugar, for dusting

Method

1 Preheat the oven to 350°F (180°C). Line the base of the pan with parchment paper. In a heatproof bowl set over a pan of simmering water, melt the butter and chocolate together until smooth and glossy, stirring now and again (make sure the base of the bowl does not touch the water).

2 Remove from the pan and allow to cool slightly, then stir in the sugar, followed by the egg yolks, one at a time.

3 Put the egg whites in a mixing bowl with the salt and whisk with an electric hand whisk until soft peaks form. Gradually fold into the chocolate mixture, then pour into the cake pan and smooth the top.

4 Bake for 1 hour, or until the top is firm but the middle still wobbles slightly when you shake the pan. Leave to cool completely in the pan. Remove the parchment paper. Dust with cocoa powder or confectioner's sugar before serving.

BAKER'S TIP
To give a deliciously moist, almost gooey finish to this recipe, be sure not to overcook the cake. The center should be only just set when it is taken out of the oven, and when pressed gently with a finger it should hold the impression and not spring back. Serve with whipped cream.

German Apple Cake

This simple apple cake is transformed into something special with a delicious, crumbly streusel topping.

SERVES 6–8
30 MINS
45–50 MINS

Chilling time
30 mins

Special equipment
8in (20cm) springform cake pan

Ingredients

For the streusel topping
1 cup all-purpose flour
½ cup light brown sugar
2 tsp ground cinnamon
6 tbsp unsalted butter, diced

For the cake
12 tbsp unsalted butter, softened, plus extra for greasing

1 cup light brown sugar
finely grated zest of 1 lemon
3 large eggs, lightly beaten
1¼ cups all-purpose flour, plus extra for dusting
1 tsp baking powder
½ tsp salt
3 tbsp milk
2 tart apples, peeled, cored, and cut into even, slim wedges

1 To make the topping, put the flour, sugar, and cinnamon in a mixing bowl.

2 Rub in the butter gently with your fingertips to form a crumbly ball of dough.

3 Wrap the streusel dough in plastic wrap and chill in the refrigerator for 30 minutes.

4 Preheat the oven to 375°F (190°C). Grease the cake pan and line with parchment paper.

5 Cream the butter and sugar with an electric mixer until pale and creamy.

6 Add the lemon zest and beat slowly until well dispersed through the batter.

7 Beat in the eggs, a little at a time, beating well after each addition to prevent curdling.

8 Sift the flour, baking powder, and salt into the bowl, then mix in to the batter.

9 Finally, add the milk to the batter and gently mix it in.

10 Spread half the mixture in the prepared pan and smooth the surface.

11 Arrange half the apple wedges over the batter, reserving the best pieces for the top.

12 Spread the rest of the batter over the apples and smooth once more with a knife.

13 Arrange the remaining apple wedges on top of the cake in an attractive pattern.

14 Remove the streusel dough from the refrigerator and coarsely grate it.

15 Sprinkle the grated streusel evenly over the top of the cake.

16 Bake in the center of the oven for 50–60 minutes. Insert a skewer into the center.

17 If the skewer emerges coated in batter, cook for a few minutes more and test again.

18 Leave the cake in the pan for 10 minutes, then carefully remove from the pan, always keeping the streusel on top, and cool on a wire rack. Serve warm.

Apple Cake variations

Apple, Raisin, and Pecan Cake

Sometimes I like a healthier cake. This cake uses little fat and is stuffed full of fruit and nuts, making it a virtuous yet delicious choice.

SERVES 10–12   **25 MINS**   **30–35 MINS**

Special equipment
9in (23cm) round springform cake pan

Ingredients
butter, for greasing
2 cups all-purpose flour, plus more for dusting
⅓ cup (2oz) shelled pecans
1⅔ cups (7oz) peeled, cored, diced apples
¾ cup light brown sugar
2 tsp baking powder
2 tsp cinnamon
1 tsp salt
¼ cup sunflower oil
¼ cup milk, plus extra if necessary
2 large eggs, at room temperature
1 tsp pure vanilla extract
⅓ cup golden raisins
whipped cream, or confectioner's sugar, to serve

Method
1 Preheat the oven to 350°F (180°C). Grease the pan and dust with flour. Place the pecans on a baking sheet and toast in the oven for 5 minutes until crisp. Cool and coarsely chop.

2 In a large bowl, mix together the apples and sugar. Sift over the flour, baking powder, cinnamon, and salt, and fold in gently. In a bowl, whisk together the oil, milk, eggs, and vanilla extract.

3 Pour the milk mixture over the flour mixture and stir until well combined. Add more milk if needed to create a dropping consistency. Fold in the nuts and raisins and pour into the pan.

4 Bake in the center of the oven for 30–35 minutes, until golden and well risen. The cake is ready when the surface is springy to the touch. Leave to cool for a few minutes in the pan, then turn out on to a wire rack. Serve warm with whipped cream, or cold and dusted with confectioner's sugar.

STORE The cake will keep in an airtight container for 3 days.

Torta di mela

A firm dessert apple is best for this moist, dense Italian cake.

SERVES 8   **20–25 MINS**   **1¼–1½ HOURS**   **UP TO 8 WEEKS**

Special equipment
9–10in (23–25cm) round springform cake pan

Ingredients
12 tbsp unsalted butter, softened
1¼ cups all-purpose flour, plus extra for dusting
½ tsp salt
1 tsp baking powder
1lb 6oz (630g) apples (about 3 medium apples)
finely grated zest and juice of 1 lemon
1 cup sugar, plus ¼ cup for glazing
2 large eggs, at room temperature
¼ cup milk

Method
1 Preheat the oven to 350°F (180°C). Grease the pan, and sprinkle with a little flour. Sift the flour with the salt and baking powder. Peel, core, and thinly slice the apples. Squeeze the lemon juice over the apples and toss well.

2 With an electric mixer, beat the butter until creamy. Add the sugar and zest, and beat until light and crumbly. Add the eggs one by one, beating well after each addition. Slowly beat in the milk until the batter is smooth.

3 Sift over the flour mixture and mix in gently. Stir in half the apple slices. Spoon the batter into the pan and smooth the top. Arrange the remaining apple slices in concentric circles on top. Bake for 1¼–1½ hours.

4 Meanwhile, make the glaze: Heat 4 tablespoons water with the sugar in a small saucepan over low heat until the sugar has dissolved. Bring to a boil and simmer for 2 minutes, without stirring, then let cool.

5 The cake is done when it shrinks slightly from the sides of the pan. Brush the sugar glaze on top of the cake, and let the cake cool in the pan. Transfer to a serving plate.

STORE The cake will keep in an airtight container for 2 days.

Toffee Apple Cake

Caramelizing the apples in this cake gives them a wonderful toffee apple taste, and soaking the cake in the buttery cooking juices after baking makes it especially moist and flavorful.

SERVES 8–10 · **40 MINS** · **40–45 MINS** · **UP TO 4 WEEKS**

Special equipment
9in (22cm) round springform cake pan

Ingredients
14 tbsp unsalted butter, softened,
  plus extra for greasing
¼ cup sugar
1⅔ cups (9oz) peeled, cored, and diced apples
  (about 1 large apple)
¾ cup light brown sugar
3 large eggs, at room temperature
1 cup all-purpose flour
1 tsp baking powder
½ tsp salt
confectioner's sugar, sifted, or whipped cream,
  to serve

Method

1 Preheat the oven to 350°F (180°C). Grease the cake pan and line the base with parchment paper. In a large frying pan, slowly melt 3 tablespoons of the butter and the sugar until the mixture is golden brown. Add the apples and cook gently for 7–8 minutes until they start to soften, brown, and take on a caramelized appearance.

2 By hand, or in an electric mixer, cream together the remaining butter and brown sugar until light and fluffy. Beat in the eggs one at a time, beating well between each addition. Sift the flour, baking powder, and salt together and fold into the egg mixture.

3 Remove the apples from the pan with a slotted spoon and set aside the pan with the juices to use later. Scatter the apples over the base of the pan. Spoon the batter on top, then place the pan on a baking sheet with sides to catch any drips, and bake in the center of the oven for 40–45 minutes. Leave to cool slightly, then transfer to a wire rack.

4 Put the frying pan with the leftover juices back over low heat, and heat gently until fully liquid. With a skewer, make holes over the surface of the cake. Put the cake on a plate and pour over the apple syrup, letting it soak in. Serve warm with whipped cream, or cooled and dusted with confectioner's sugar.

STORE The cake will keep in an airtight container for 3 days.

Rhubarb and Ginger Upside Down Cake

Young rhubarb is cooked into a simple upside down cake to give a modern twist on a classic dessert.

SERVES 6–8 | **40 MINS** | **40–45 MINS**

Special equipment
9in (22cm) round springform cake pan

Ingredients
11 tbsp unsalted butter, softened, plus extra for greasing
1lb 2oz (500g) young, pink rhubarb
¾ cup dark brown sugar
4 tbsp finely chopped preserved ginger in syrup
3 large eggs, at room temperature
1 cup all-purpose flour
2 tsp ground ginger
1¼ tsp baking powder
½ tsp salt
heavy cream, whipped, or crème fraîche, to serve

1 Preheat the oven to 350°F (180°C). Grease the cake pan with the softened butter.

2 Line the base and sides of the cake pan with parchment paper.

3 Wash the rhubarb, removing discolored pieces and the dry ends of the stalks.

4 Cut the rhubarb into even-sized ¾in (2cm) lengths with a sharp knife.

5 Scatter a little of the sugar evenly over the base of the cake pan.

6 Now scatter half the chopped ginger evenly over the base of the pan.

7 Lay the rhubarb in the pan, tightly packed, making sure the base is well covered.

8 Place the butter and remaining sugar into a large bowl.

9 With an electric mixer, cream the butter and sugar until light and fluffy, about 2 minutes.

10 Beat in the eggs one at a time, beating as much air as possible into the mixture.

11 Gently mix the remaining chopped ginger into the cake batter, until well dispersed.

12 Sift the flour, ground ginger, baking powder, and salt into a separate large bowl.

13 Add the sifted ingredients to the bowl containing the cake batter.

14 Gently mix the sifted dry ingredients into the wet ingredients, keeping the batter's volume.

15 Spoon the cake batter over the rhubarb base, being careful not to disturb the rhubarb.

16 Bake the cake in the center of the oven for 45 minutes until the surface is springy.

17 Leave the cake to cool in its pan for 20–30 minutes, before carefully turning it out.

18 Serve warm as a dessert with whipped cream or crème fraîche. **STORE** The cake is also good cold and will keep in a cool place in an airtight container for 2 days.

Fresh Fruit Cake variations

Blueberry Upside Down Cake

This is an unusual yet delicious way of turning a basket of blueberries and a few pantry essentials into a quick and delicious dessert for a crowd.

SERVES 8–10 **15 MINS** **40–50 MINS**

Special equipment
9in (22cm) round springform cake pan

Ingredients
11 tbsp unsalted butter, softened, plus extra for greasing
⅔ cup sugar
3 large eggs, at room temperature
1 tsp pure vanilla extract
¾ cup all-purpose flour
1 tsp baking powder
½ tsp salt
⅓ cup ground almonds
2¼ cups (9oz) fresh or frozen blueberries
confectioner's sugar, to serve

Method
1 Preheat the oven to 350°F (180°C) and place a baking sheet inside. Grease the cake pan and line the base with parchment paper. By hand, or in an electric mixer, cream together the butter and sugar until light and fluffy.

2 Gradually beat in the eggs and vanilla extract, beating well between each addition, until well combined. Sift over the flour, baking powder, and salt and mix it in gently. Gently mix in the ground almonds.

3 Place the blueberries into the bottom of the prepared cake pan, ensuring there is an even layer. Spread the batter over the berries, taking care not to dislodge them.

4 Bake the cake on the baking sheet in the center of the oven for 40–50 minutes until golden brown and springy to the touch; a skewer inserted into the middle of the cake should come out clean. Leave to cool in the pan for a few minutes, before loosening the sides and gently lifting off the pan base and parchment paper.

5 Place the cake on a serving plate. Dust with confectioner's sugar and serve cold, or serve warm as a dessert with heavy cream or light vanilla custard.

STORE The cake will keep for 2 days in an airtight container.

Pear Cake

Fresh pear, yogurt, and almonds make this a very moist cake.

SERVES 6–8 **40 MINS** **45–50 MINS** **UP TO 8 WEEKS**

Special equipment
8in (20cm) round springform cake pan

Ingredients
7 tbsp unsalted butter, softened
¾ cup all-purpose flour, plus extra for dusting
⅓ cup light brown sugar
1 egg, at room temperature, lightly beaten
1 tsp baking powder
½ tsp ground ginger
½ tsp cinnamon
½ tsp salt
finely grated zest and juice of ½ orange
¼ cup Greek yogurt, or sour cream
¼ cup ground almonds
1 large pear, peeled, cored, and finely sliced
confectioner's sugar, to dust

For the topping
2 tbsp toasted almond flakes
2 tbsp demerara sugar

Method
1 Preheat the oven to 350°F (180°C). Grease the cake pan and dust with flour. Cream the butter and sugar with an electric mixer or by hand until fluffy. Beat the egg into the creamed mixture.

2 Sift together the flour, baking powder, ground ginger, cinnamon, and salt and mix into the creamed mixture. Mix in the orange zest and juice, yogurt or sour cream, then the almonds. Spread half the cake batter into the pan. Top with the pears and cover with the other half of the batter.

3 In a small bowl, toss together the almond flakes and demerara sugar. Sprinkle the mixture over the top of the cake and bake in the center of the oven for 45–50 minutes.

4 Leave the cake to cool in its pan for about 10 minutes, then turn it out to cool on a wire rack. Serve warm or at room temperature.

STORE The cake will keep in a cool place in an airtight container for 3 days.

Cherry and Almond Cake

A classic combination of flavors, always popular with guests.

SERVES 8–10 | **20 MINS** | **1½–1¾ HOURS** | **UP TO 4 WEEKS**

Special equipment
8in (20cm) deep round springform cake pan

Ingredients
11 tbsp unsalted butter, softened
1¾ cups all-purpose flour, sifted
⅔ cup sugar
2 large eggs, at room temperature, lightly beaten
2 tsp baking powder
1 tsp salt
1⅓ cups (6oz) ground almonds
1 tsp pure vanilla extract
⅓ cup whole milk
14oz (400g) pitted cherries
¼ cup (scant 1oz) whole blanched almonds, chopped (lengthwise looks pretty)

Method
1 Preheat the oven to 350°F (180°C). Lightly grease the cake pan and dust with flour. In a bowl, beat the butter and sugar with an electric hand mixer until creamy. Beat in the eggs one at a time, adding 1 tablespoon of the flour before adding the second egg.

2 Mix in the remaining flour, the baking powder, salt, ground almonds, and vanilla extract. Stir in the milk and mix in half the cherries, then spoon the mixture into the pan and smooth the top. Scatter the remaining cherries over the surface, followed by the almonds.

3 Bake for 1½–1¾ hours, or until golden and firm to the touch. The exact cooking time will depend on how juicy the cherries are. If the surface of the cake starts to brown too much before it is fully cooked, cover with foil. When cooked, cool in the pan for a few minutes and transfer to a wire rack to cool completely before serving.

STORE This cake will keep in an airtight container for 2 days.

Bavarian Plum Cake

Bavaria is famous for its sweet baking. This unusual cake is a cross between a sweet bread and a custard fruit tart.

SERVES 8–10	35–40 MINS	50–55 MINS	UP TO 4 WEEKS

Rising and proofing time
2–2¾ hrs

Special equipment
11in (28cm) tart pan

Ingredients

For the brioche dough
1½ tsp dried yeast
vegetable oil, for greasing

2¾ cups all-purpose flour
2 tbsp sugar
1 tsp salt
3 large eggs, at room temperature
9 tbsp unsalted butter, plus
   extra for greasing

For the filling
2 tbsp dried bread crumbs
1lb 12½oz (875g) plums, pitted
   and quartered
2 large egg yolks
½ cup sugar
¼ cup heavy cream

Method

1 Sprinkle the yeast over ¼ cup lukewarm water in a small bowl. Let stand for 5 minutes, until dissolved. Lightly oil another bowl. Sift the flour on to a work surface. Make a well in the center and add the sugar, salt, yeast mixture, and eggs.

2 Work in the flour to form a soft dough, adding more flour if it is very sticky. Knead on a floured work surface for 10 minutes, until very elastic. Work in more flour as needed so that the dough is slightly sticky but peels easily from the work surface.

3 Pound the butter with a rolling pin to soften it. Add the butter to the dough; pinch and squeeze to mix it in, then knead until smooth. Shape into a ball and put it into the oiled bowl. Cover, and let rise in the refrigerator for 1½–2 hours, or overnight, until doubled in bulk.

4 Grease the tart pan. Knead the chilled brioche dough lightly to knock out the air. Flour the work surface; roll out the dough into a 13in (32cm) round. Wrap the dough around the rolling pin and loosely drape it over the dish. Press the dough into the dish,

and cut off any excess. Sprinkle the bread crumbs over the dough. Preheat the oven to 425°F (220°C). Put a baking sheet in the oven to heat.

5 Arrange the plum wedges, cut side up, in concentric circles on the brioche shell. Let stand at room temperature for 30–45 minutes, until the dough is puffed.

6 Put the egg yolks and two-thirds of the sugar into a bowl. Pour in the heavy cream, whisk together, and set aside.

7 Sprinkle the plum wedges with the remaining sugar and bake the tart on the baking sheet for 5 minutes. Reduce the heat to 350°F (180°C). Ladle the custard mixture over the fruit, return the tart to the oven, and continue baking for 45–50 minutes longer, until the dough is browned, the fruit tender, and the custard just set. Let cool on a wire rack. Serve warm or at room temperature.

STORE The tart will keep in an airtight container in the fridge for 2 days.

BAKER'S TIP

Baked custard should never be completely set when it is taken from the oven; instead, there should always be a slight wobble in the center when the pan is shaken, or the custard will be rubbery and hard rather than unctuous and yielding.

Banana Bread

Ripe bananas are delicious baked in this sweet quick bread. Spices and nuts add flavor and crunch.

MAKES 2 LOAVES | **20–25 MINS** | **35–40 MINS** | **UP TO 8 WEEKS**

Special equipment
2 x (8½ x 4½ x 2½in/21.5 x 11 x 6cm/1lb) loaf pans

Ingredients
unsalted butter, for greasing
2¾ cups all-purpose flour, plus extra for dusting
2 tsp baking powder
2 tsp cinnamon
1 tsp salt
1 cup (4oz) walnut pieces, coarsely chopped
3 large eggs, at room temperature
3 ripe bananas, peeled and chopped
finely grated zest and juice of 1 lemon
½ cup vegetable oil
1 cup sugar
½ cup brown sugar
2 tsp pure vanilla extract

1 Preheat the oven to 350°F (180°C). Grease each of the loaf pans thoroughly.

2 Sprinkle 2–3 tablespoons flour into each pan and turn to coat, then tap to remove excess.

3 Sift the flour, baking powder, cinnamon, and salt into a large bowl. Mix in the walnuts.

4 Make a well in the center of the flour mixture for the wet ingredients.

5 With a fork, beat the eggs in a separate bowl just until mixed.

6 Mash the bananas in another bowl with a fork until they form a smooth paste.

7 Stir the bananas into the egg until well blended. Add the lemon zest and mix well.

8 Add the oil, both sugars, vanilla, and lemon juice. Stir until thoroughly combined.

9 Pour ¾ of the banana mixture into the well in the flour and stir well.

10 Gradually draw in the dry ingredients, adding the remaining banana mixture.

11 Stir until just smooth; if the batter is over-mixed, the banana bread will be tough.

12 Spoon the batter into the prepared pans. The pans should be about half full.

13 Bake for 35–40 minutes, until the loaves start to shrink from the sides of the pans.

14 Test the loaves with a metal skewer inserted in the center; it should come out clean.

15 Let the loaves cool slightly, then transfer to a wire rack to cool completely.

16 Serve the banana bread sliced and spread with cream cheese, or toasted and buttered.
STORE Banana bread will keep in an airtight container for 3–4 days.

Loaf Cake variations

Apple Loaf Cake

Here, apples and whole wheat flour make for a healthier cake.

| MAKES 1 LOAF | 30 MINS | 40–50 MINS | UP TO 8 WEEKS |

Special equipment
9 x 5in (23 x 12cm) loaf pan

Ingredients
8 tbsp unsalted butter, softened,
  plus extra for greasing
½ cup all-purpose flour, plus extra for dusting
⅓ cup light brown sugar
¼ cup sugar
2 large eggs
1 tsp pure vanilla extract
½ cup whole wheat flour
1 tsp baking powder
¼ tsp salt
2 tsp cinnamon
2 apples, peeled, cored, and diced

Method
1 Preheat the oven to 350°F (180°C). Grease the pan and dust the base with flour. In a bowl, whisk together the butter and the sugars.

2 Beat in the eggs, one at a time. Add the vanilla extract. In a separate bowl, sift together the flours, baking powder, salt, and cinnamon. Fold the dry ingredients into the batter, mixing well.

3 Toss the apples in a little all-purpose flour, then fold them into the batter. Pour the mixture into the pan. Bake in the center of the oven for 40–50 minutes, until the cake is golden brown. Leave to cool slightly then turn out onto a wire rack.

STORE The cake will keep in an airtight container for 3 days.

> **BAKER'S TIP**
> When baking with any dried or fresh fruit, toss it lightly in flour before adding it to the wet ingredients. This floury coating will help stop the fruit from sinking to the bottom of the cake while cooking, ensuring it stays evenly distributed throughout.

Pecan and Cranberry Loaf Cake

Dried cranberries make a novel alternative to the more commonly used raisins, adding sweet and sharp notes to this wholesome cake. ▶

| MAKES 1 LOAF | 30 MINS | 50–60 MINS | UP TO 4 WEEKS |

Special equipment
9 x 5in (23 x 12cm) loaf pan

Ingredients
7 tbsp unsalted butter, plus extra for greasing
1¾ cups all-purpose flour, plus extra for dusting
½ cup light brown sugar
½ cup dried cranberries, coarsely chopped
⅓ cup pecans, coarsely chopped
finely grated zest and juice of 1 orange
2 large eggs, at room temperature
½ cup milk
2 tsp baking powder
1 tsp salt
½ tsp cinnamon
¾ cup confectioner's sugar, sifted

Method
1 Preheat the oven to 350°F (180°C). Grease the loaf pan and dust with flour. In a saucepan, melt the butter. Leave to cool slightly, then stir in the sugar, cranberries, pecans, and zest of 1 orange. Whisk together the eggs and milk, then stir them in as well.

2 In a separate bowl, sift together the flour, baking powder, salt, and cinnamon. Fold into the batter, mixing well. Pour into the pan, then bake in the center of the oven for 50–60 minutes. Leave to cool slightly, then turn out.

3 Mix the confectioner's sugar and remaining zest. Add enough orange juice for a drizzling consistency. Drizzle the icing over the cooled cake and let dry before slicing.

STORE Will keep in a container for 3 days.

Sweet Potato Bread

Savory sounding, this is very much a sweet cake and similar to a banana bread in looks and texture.

| MAKES 1 LOAF | 10 MINS | 1 HOUR | UP TO 4 WEEKS |

Special equipment
9 x 5in (23 x 12cm) loaf pan

Ingredients
7 tbsp unsalted butter, softened, plus extra
  for greasing
1½ cups all-purpose flour, plus more for dusting
6oz (175g) sweet potatoes, peeled and diced
2 tsp baking powder
pinch of salt
½ tsp pumpkin pie spice
½ tsp cinnamon
⅔ cup sugar
½ cup pecans, coarsely chopped
½ cup chopped dates
2 large eggs
½ cup sunflower or vegetable oil

Method
1 Grease the pan and dust with flour, knocking out any excess. Place the sweet potatoes in a saucepan, cover with water, and bring to a boil. Simmer for 10 minutes, until tender. Mash and set aside to cool.

2 Preheat the oven to 335°F (170°C). In a large bowl, sift together the flour, baking powder, salt, spices, and sugar. Add the pecans and dates and mix in thoroughly. Make a well in the center.

3 In a large measuring cup, whisk the eggs with the oil until emulsified. Stir in the potatoes until smooth. Pour into the flour mix and stir until well combined with no lumps.

4 Pour the batter into the loaf pan and smooth the top with a palette knife. Bake in the center of the oven for 1 hour, until well risen and a skewer comes out clean. Leave to cool for 5 minutes before turning out.

STORE The cake will keep in an airtight container for 3 days.

celebration cakes

Rich Fruit Cake

This recipe makes a wonderfully moist, rich fruit cake, ideal for Christmas, weddings, christenings, or birthdays.

SERVES 16 · **25 MINS** · **2½ HOURS**

Soaking time
overnight

Special equipment
Deep 8–10in (20–25cm) cake pan

Ingredients

1¼ cups (7oz) golden raisins
2½ (14oz) cups raisins
2 cups (12oz) prunes, chopped
2½ cups (12oz) glacé cherries
2 small apples, peeled, cored, and finely chopped
2 cups cider
4 tsp pumpkin pie spice

14 tbsp unsalted butter, softened
1 cup dark brown sugar
3 large eggs, beaten
1⅓ cups (6oz) ground almonds
2 cups all-purpose flour
2 tsp baking powder
14oz (400g) store-bought marzipan
2–3 tbsp apricot jam

4 cups confectioner's sugar, plus extra for dusting
3 large egg whites

1 Place the golden raisins, raisins, prunes, cherries, apple, cider, and spice in a saucepan.

2 Bring slowly to simmer over medium-low heat, cover, and simmer for 20 minutes.

3 Remove from the heat. Leave overnight at room temperature; the fruits will absorb liquid.

4 Preheat the oven to 325°F (160°C). Double-line the cake pan with parchment paper.

5 Cream the butter and sugar with an electric mixer until fluffy, about 2 minutes.

6 Add the eggs, a little at a time, beating very well after each addition to prevent curdling.

7 Gently mix in the fruit and ground almonds, trying to keep the volume in the batter.

8 Sift the flour and baking powder into a large bowl, and mix into the batter.

9 Spoon the batter into the prepared pan, cover with foil, and bake for 2½ hours.

10 Test if the cake is ready: a skewer inserted into the center should come out clean.

11 Leave to cool, then turn out on a wire rack to cool completely. Remove the parchment paper.

12 Trim the cake to level it. Transfer to a stand and hold in place with some marzipan.

13 Warm the jam and brush thickly over the whole cake. This will help the marzipan stick.

14 On a lightly floured surface, knead the remaining marzipan until softened.

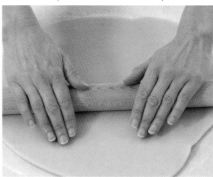

15 Roll out the softened marzipan until wide enough to cover the cake.

16 Wrap the marzipan around the rolling pin, and drape it over the cold fruit cake.

17 Gently, with your hands, ease the marzipan into place, smoothing out any bumps.

18 With a small, sharp knife, cut away any excess marzipan from the base of the cake.

19 Place the egg whites in a bowl and sift in the confectioner's sugar. Stir well to combine.

20 With an electric mixer, beat the sugar mixture for 10 minutes until stiff.

21 Spread the icing with a palette knife.
STORE Will keep, un-iced, for 8 weeks.

Fruit Cake variations

Prune Chocolate Dessert Cake

Soaked prunes give this rich, dark cake a warming depth of flavor, making it a perfect dessert for the winter months.

| SERVES 8–10 | 30 MINS | 40–45 MINS | UP TO 8 WEEKS |

Soaking time
overnight

Special equipment
9in (22cm) round springform cake pan

Ingredients
½ cup (4oz) prunes, coarsely chopped
½ cup brandy, or cold black tea
9 tbsp unsalted butter, diced,
  plus extra for greasing
9oz good-quality dark chocolate, at least 60%
  cocoa solids
3 large eggs, at room temperature, separated
⅔ cup sugar
1 cup (4oz) ground almonds
cocoa powder, sifted, to dust

Method
1 Soak the prunes in the brandy or tea overnight. When ready to bake, preheat the oven to 350°F (180°C). Grease the pan and line the base with parchment paper.

2 Melt the chocolate and butter over a pan of gently simmering water; do not let the base of the bowl touch the water. Cool. Whisk together the egg yolks and sugar with an electric hand mixer. Whisk the egg whites separately to soft peaks.

3 Mix the cooled chocolate into the egg yolk mixture. Fold in the ground almonds, prunes, and their soaking liquid, and mix until well combined. Beat 2 tablespoons of the egg whites into the cake batter. Gently fold in the remaining egg whites.

4 Pour the mixture into the pan, smooth the top, and bake in the center of the oven for 40–45 minutes. The center will still be slightly soft. Leave the cake to cool for a few minutes in its pan, then turn it out on to a wire rack.

5 Serve the cake upside down. Dust with cocoa powder and serve with crème fraîche.

STORE This will keep in an airtight container for 5 days.

Tea Bread

A simple recipe; don't forget to use the soaking water as well as the fruit.

| SERVES 8–10 | 20 MINS | 1 HOUR | UP TO 4 WEEKS |

Soaking time
overnight

Special equipment
9 x 5½in (23 x 13cm) loaf pan

Ingredients
1¾ cups (9oz) mixed dried fruit (golden raisins,
  raisins, currants, and mixed citrus peel)
½ cup light brown sugar
1 cup cold black tea
unsalted butter, for greasing
1½ cups all-purpose flour, plus more for dusting
½ cup (2oz) walnuts or hazelnuts, chopped
1 large egg, beaten
1½ tsp baking powder
½ tsp salt

Method
1 Mix the dried fruit and sugar together and leave to soak in the cold tea overnight. When ready to bake, preheat the oven to 350°F (180°C). Grease the loaf pan and dust with flour.

2 Add the nuts and the egg to the fruit mixture, and mix well to combine. Sift over the flour, baking powder, and salt, and mix in thoroughly.

3 Bake in the center of the oven for about 1 hour, until the top is dark golden brown and springy to the touch, and a skewer inserted into the center comes out clean.

4 Leave to cool for a few minutes in the pan, then turn out to cool completely on a wire rack. This is best served sliced or toasted with butter.

STORE The bread will keep in an airtight container for 5 days.

Light Fruit Cake

Not everyone enjoys a classic rich fruit cake, especially after a hearty celebration meal. This lighter version is a quick and easy alternative that's less heavy on the fruit.

SERVES 8–12 | **25 MINS** | **1¾ HOURS** | **UP TO 8 WEEKS**

Special equipment
Deep 8in (20cm) round cake pan

Ingredients
12 tbsp unsalted butter, softened
1 cup light brown sugar
3 large eggs, at room temperature
1¾ cups all-purpose flour, sifted
2 tsp baking powder
1 tsp salt
2–3 tbsp milk
2 cups (10oz) mixed dried fruit such as figs, pineapple, cherries if possible

Method
1 Preheat the oven to 350°F (180°C). Line the base and sides of the pan with parchment paper. In a bowl, beat the butter and sugar together with an electric hand mixer until creamy, then beat in the eggs, one at a time, adding a little of the flour after each. Mix in the remaining flour, baking powder, salt, and the milk; the mixture should drop easily from the beaters. Add the dried fruit and mix in until well combined.

2 Spoon the mixture into the pan, level the top, and bake for 1½–1¾ hours, or until firm to the touch and a skewer inserted into the middle of the cake comes out clean. Leave in the pan to cool completely. Remove the parchment paper.

STORE This will keep in an airtight container for 3 days.

Plum Pudding

So-named because it contains prunes, this is a classic Christmas dish, here using butter instead of the traditional beef suet.

SERVES 8–10	45 MINS	8–10 HOURS	UP TO 1 YEAR

Soaking time
overnight

Special equipment
2¼lb (1kg) pudding bowl or 1 quart bowl

Ingredients
½ cup (3oz) raisins
½ cup (2oz) currants
⅔ cup (4oz) golden raisins
¼ cup (2oz) mixed citrus peel, chopped
1 cup (4oz) mixed dried fruit, such as figs, dates, and cherries, chopped
⅔ cup beer
1 tbsp whisky or brandy
finely grated zest and juice of 1 orange
finely grated zest and juice of 1 lemon
½ cup (3oz) pitted prunes, chopped
⅔ cup cold black tea
1 apple, grated
8 tbsp unsalted butter, melted, plus extra for greasing
1 cup dark brown sugar
1 tbsp unsulfured light molasses
2 large eggs, at room temperature, beaten
½ cup all-purpose flour
1 tsp pumpkin pie spice
½ tsp baking powder
¼ tsp salt
1 cup (4oz) fresh white bread crumbs
⅓ cup (2oz) chopped almonds

Method

1 Put the first 9 ingredients into a large bowl and mix well. Put the prunes in a small bowl and pour in the tea. Cover the bowls, then leave to soak overnight.

2 Drain the prunes and discard any remaining tea. Add the prunes and the apple to the rest of the fruit, followed by the butter, sugar, molasses, and eggs. Stir well.

3 Sift in the flour with the pumpkin pie spice, baking powder, and salt, then stir the bread crumbs and almonds into the mixture. Mix together well until all the ingredients are thoroughly combined.

4 Grease the pudding bowl and pour in the mixture. Cover with 2 layers of parchment paper and 1 layer of foil. Tie the layers to the bowl with string, then put the bowl on a rack in a large deep pan of simmering water that comes at least halfway up the side. Cover tightly and steam for 8–10 hours.

5 Check regularly to make sure that the water level does not drop too low. Serve with brandy butter, cream, or custard.

STORE If well sealed, the pudding will keep for up to 1 year in a cool place.

BAKER'S TIP

When steaming a pudding for an extended time, it is very important that the water level in the pan should not drop too low. There are a couple of easy ways to avoid this. Either set a timer every hour, to remind you to check the water level, or put a marble in the pan so it rattles when the water level drops.

Stollen

This rich, fruity sweet bread, originally from Germany, is traditionally served at Christmas and makes a great alternative to Christmas cakes or pies.

| SERVES 12 | 30 MINS | 50 MINS | UP TO 4 WEEKS |

Soaking time
overnight

Rising and proofing time
2–3 hours

Ingredients
1¼ cup (7oz) raisins
¾ cup (4oz) currants
½ cup rum
3 cups all-purpose flour, plus extra for dusting
1 (¼oz/10g) package dried yeast
¼ cup sugar
½ cup milk
few drops of pure vanilla extract
pinch of salt
½ tsp pumpkin pie spice
2 large eggs, at room temperature
12 tbsp unsalted butter, softened
7oz (200g) mixed candied citrus peel
1 cup (4oz) ground almonds
confectioner's sugar, for dusting

Method

1 Put the raisins and currants into a medium bowl, pour in the rum, and leave the ingredients to soak overnight.

2 The following day, sift the flour into a large bowl, make a well in the center, sprinkle in the yeast, and add 1 teaspoon of the sugar. Gently heat the milk until lukewarm and pour on top of the yeast. Let stand at room temperature for 15 minutes, or until frothy.

3 Add the rest of the sugar, the vanilla extract, salt, pumpkin pie spice, eggs, and butter. Using a wooden spoon, or electric mixer with a dough hook, mix, then knead the ingredients together for 5 minutes, or until they form a smooth dough.

4 Transfer to a lightly floured work surface. Add the candied peel, soaked raisins and currants, and almonds, kneading for a few minutes until incorporated. Return the dough to the bowl, cover with plastic wrap, and let rise in a warm place until doubled in size.

5 Preheat the oven to 325°F (160°C). Line a baking sheet with parchment paper. On a floured surface, roll out the dough to make a 12 x 10in (30 x 25cm) rectangle. Fold 1 long side over, just beyond the middle, then fold over the other long side to overlap the first, curling it over slightly on top to create the stollen shape. Transfer to the baking sheet, and put in a warm place to rise again until doubled in size.

6 Bake in the oven for 50 minutes, or until risen and pale golden. Transfer to a wire rack to cool completely, then generously dust with confectioner's sugar. Serve cut into thick slices, with or without butter.

STORE The stollen will keep in an airtight container for 4 days.

BAKER'S TIP
Stollen can be made with any combination of dried fruits. It can be plain, as in this recipe, or stuffed with a marzipan or frangipane layer. Any leftovers are great for breakfast, lightly toasted, with butter.

Chocolate Chestnut Roulade

Perfect for a winter celebration, this rolled sponge is filled with a rich chestnut purée mixed with whipped cream.

SERVES 8–10

50–55 MINS

5–7 MINS

8 WEEKS, UNFILLED

Special equipment
17 x 11in (43 x 28cm) baking sheet
piping bag and star nozzle

Ingredients
butter, for greasing
¼ cup cocoa powder
1 tbsp all-purpose flour
pinch of salt
5 large eggs, separated
⅔ cup sugar

For the filling
4oz (125g) chestnut purée
2 tbsp dark rum
⅔ cup heavy cream
1oz (30g) dark chocolate,
  finely chopped
sugar to taste (optional)

To finish and decorate
¼ cup sugar
2 tbsp dark rum
½ cup heavy cream
2oz (50g) dark chocolate, grated

1 Preheat the oven to 425°F (220°C). Grease a baking sheet. Line with parchment paper.

2 Sift the cocoa powder, flour, and salt into a large bowl and set aside.

3 Beat the egg yolks with ⅔ of the sugar; it should leave a ribbon trail.

4 Whisk the egg whites until stiff. Sprinkle in the remaining sugar and whisk again until glossy.

5 Sift ⅓ of the cocoa mixture over the yolk mixture. Add ⅓ of the egg whites.

6 Fold together lightly. Add the remaining cocoa mixture and egg white in 2 batches.

7 Pour the batter onto the prepared baking sheet. Spread the batter almost to the edges.

8 Bake in the bottom of the oven for 5–7 minutes. The cake will be risen and just firm.

9 Remove the cake from the oven, invert onto a damp towel, and peel off the parchment paper.

10 Tightly roll up the cake around the damp kitchen towel and leave to cool.

11 Put the chestnut purée in a bowl with the rum. Whip the cream until it forms soft peaks.

12 Melt the chocolate in a bowl over a pot of simmering water. Stir into the chestnut mixture.

13 Fold the chocolate and chestnut mixture into the whipped cream. Add sugar to taste.

14 To finish, simmer half the sugar in ¼ cup of water for 1 minute. Cool and stir in the rum.

15 Unroll the cake on fresh parchment paper. Brush with syrup and spread the chestnut mix.

16 Using the parchment underneath, carefully roll up the filled cake as tightly as possible.

17 Whip the cream and remaining sugar until stiff. Fill the piping bag with the cream.

18 With a serrated knife, trim each end of the cake diagonally. Transfer to a serving plate. Decorate with the whipped cream and chocolate shavings. Best eaten on the day it is made.

Chocolate Roulade variations

Chocolate Log

A roulade with the classic pairing of dark chocolate and raspberry.

SERVES 10	30 MINS	15 MINS	UP TO 24 WEEKS

Special equipment
8 x 12in (20 x 30cm) jelly roll pan

Ingredients
3 large eggs, at room temperature
⅓ cup sugar
½ cup all-purpose flour
3 tbsp cocoa powder
½ tsp baking powder
¾ cup heavy cream
5oz (140g) dark chocolate, chopped
3 tbsp raspberry jam
confectioner's sugar, for dusting

Method
1 Preheat the oven to 350°F (180°C). Line the pan with parchment paper.

2 In a bowl, whisk the eggs with the sugar and 1 tablespoon water for 5 minutes, until light; the mixture should hold a trail. Sift the flour, cocoa powder, and baking powder over the beaten eggs, then quickly fold in.

3 Pour the cake mixture into the lined pan and bake for 12 minutes. Turn it out on to a new piece of parchment paper. Peel the paper from the base of the cake and discard. Roll the cake up, while still hot, keeping the paper inside. Leave to cool.

4 Meanwhile, to make the frosting, pour the cream into a saucepan, bring to a boil, then remove from the heat. Add the chopped chocolate and leave it to melt, stirring occasionally, so it cools and thickens.

5 Carefully unroll the cake and spread raspberry jam over the surface. Spread ⅓ of the frosting over the raspberry jam, and roll it up again. Place the roll on a board, seam-side down. Spread the rest of the frosting over the the cake. Transfer to a serving plate. Just before serving, dust with confectioner's sugar.

STORE The cake will keep, chilled, for 2 days.

Chocolate Amaretti Roulade

Crushed Amaretti cookies add texture and crunch to this beautiful and indulgent roulade.

SERVES 6–8	25–30 MINS	20 MINS	8 WEEKS, UNFILLED

Special equipment
8 x 12in (20 x 30cm) jelly roll pan

Ingredients
6 large eggs (at room temperature), separated
⅔ cup sugar
½ cup cocoa powder
confectioner's sugar, for dusting
1¼ cups heavy whipping cream
2–3 tbsp Amaretto or brandy
20 Amaretti cookies, crushed, plus 2 for topping
2oz (50g) dark chocolate

Method
1 Preheat the oven to 350°F (180°C). Line the pan with parchment paper. Put the egg yolks and sugar in a large bowl set over a pan of simmering water and whisk vigorously with a balloon whisk or an electric hand mixer until pale, thick, and creamy. This will take about 10 minutes. Remove from the heat.

2 Put the egg whites in a large bowl and whisk until soft peaks form. Sift the cocoa powder into the egg yolk mixture and fold in along with the egg whites. Pour into the pan and bake for 20 minutes, or until just firm to the touch. Allow the pan to cool slightly before turning the cake out face down on to a sheet of parchment paper dusted with confectioner's sugar. Remove the pan, but leave the parchment. Let cool for 30 minutes.

3 Whisk the cream with an electric hand mixer until soft peaks form. Peel the parchment paper from the cake and place it underneath. Trim the sides, then drizzle with the Amaretto or brandy. Spread with the cream, scatter with the crushed cookies, and grate most of the chocolate over the top.

4 Starting from one of the short sides, roll the roulade up. Place on a serving plate with the seam underneath. Crumble over the extra cookies, grate with the remaining chocolate, and dust with confectioner's sugar.

Chocolate and Buttercream Roll

This chocolatey variation on a Swiss roll is simple to make and always a hit with kids—perfect for a children's party.

SERVES 8–10	20–25 MINS	10 MINS

Special equipment
8 x 12in (20 x 30cm) jelly roll pan

Ingredients
3 large eggs, at room temperature
⅓ cup sugar
¼ cup all-purpose flour
¼ cup cocoa powder, plus extra to dust
5 tbsp butter, softened
1 cup confectioner's sugar

Method
1 Preheat the oven to 400°F (200°C) and line the pan with parchment paper. Sit a bowl over a pot of simmering water, add the eggs and sugar, and whisk for 5–10 minutes, until thick and creamy. Remove from the heat, sift in the flour and cocoa, and fold in.

2 Pour into the pan and bake for 10 minutes, or until springy to the touch. Cover with a damp kitchen towel and let cool. Turn the cake out, face down, onto a sheet of parchment paper dusted with cocoa powder. Peel off the parchment paper it was baked on.

3 Whisk the butter until creamy. Beat in the confectioner's sugar, a little at a time, then spread the mixture over the cake. Using the parchment paper to help you, roll the cake up, starting from one of the ends. Dust with more cocoa powder, if needed, and serve.

STORE The cake will keep, chilled, for 3 days.

Black Forest Gâteau

Newly resurrected to its glorious best, this classic German cake deserves its place on a celebration table.

SERVES 8 | 55 MINS | 40 MINS | UP TO 4 WEEKS

Ingredients

6 tbsp butter, melted
6 large eggs, at room temperature
¾ cup sugar
¾ cup all-purpose flour
½ cup cocoa powder,
  plus more for dusting
1 tsp pure vanilla extract

For the filling and decoration

2 x 14oz (425g) cans pitted black
  cherries, drained, 6 tbsp juice reserved
  and cherries from 1 can coarsely
  chopped
4 tbsp Kirsch
2 cups heavy cream
6oz (150g) dark chocolate, grated

Special equipment

9in (23cm) springform cake pan
piping bag with star-shaped nozzle

1 Preheat the oven to 350°F (180°C). Grease and line the pan with parchment paper.

2 Put the eggs and sugar into a large heatproof bowl that will fit over a saucepan.

3 Place the bowl over a pot of simmering water. Don't let the bowl touch the water.

4 Whisk until the mixture is pale and thick, and will hold a trail from the beaters.

5 Remove from the heat and whisk for another 5 minutes, or until cooled slightly.

6 Sift the flour and cocoa together, and gently fold into the egg mixture using a spatula.

7 Fold in the vanilla and butter. Transfer to the prepared pan and level the surface.

8 Bake in the oven for 40 minutes, or until risen and just shrinking away from the sides.

9 Turn out on to a wire rack, discard the paper, and cover with a clean cloth. Let it cool.

10 Carefully cut the cake into 3 layers. Use a serrated knife and long sweeping strokes.

11 Combine the reserved cherry juice with the Kirsch, and drizzle a third over each layer.

12 Whip the cream in a separate bowl until it just holds its shape; it should not be stiff.

13 Place a layer of cake on a plate. Spread with cream and half the chopped cherries.

14 Repeat with the second sponge. Top with the final sponge, baked side up. Press down.

15 Spread the sides with a thin layer of the cream. Transfer the rest to the piping bag.

16 Press grated chocolate onto the creamy sides with a palette knife.

17 Pipe a ring of cream swirls around the cake and place the whole cherries inside.

18 Sprinkle any remaining chocolate evenly over the peaks of piped cream before serving.
STORE The cake can be covered and chilled for up to 3 days.

Gâteau variations

German Cream Cheese Torte

This German dessert is a cross between a cheesecake and a sponge cake. It makes a good party dessert as it can be made in advance.

SERVES 8–10 **40 MINS** **30 MINS**

Chilling time
3 hrs, or overnight

Special equipment
9in (22cm) springform pan

Ingredients
11 tbsp unsalted butter, softened,
   or soft margarine, plus extra for greasing
1 cup sugar
3 large eggs
1 cup all-purpose flour
1 tsp baking powder
juice of 2 lemons and finely grated zest of 1
1 tbsp unflavored powdered gelatin
1 cup heavy cream
1 cup (9oz) quark, or see Baker's Tip
confectioner's sugar, for dusting

Method

1 Preheat the oven to 350°F (180°C). Grease the pan and dust with flour.

2 Cream the butter or margarine and ⅔ cup sugar together. Beat in the eggs, one at a time, until the mixture is smooth and creamy. Sift together the flour and baking powder, and fold into the batter with the zest. Spoon into the pan and bake for 30 minutes, or until well risen. Turn the cake out onto a wire rack. Slice it in half horizontally with a serrated knife. Allow it to cool completely.

3 To make the filling, heat the lemon juice in a small pan, then remove from the heat. Add the gelatin to the lemon juice. Stir until dissolved, then let cool.

4 Whisk the cream until firm. Beat together the quark, zest, and the remaining sugar, then beat in the lemon juice and gelatin. Fold in the cream.

5 Spoon the filling onto one cake half. Slice the second half into eight pieces and arrange on top of the filling; pre-cutting the top layer makes it easier to serve. Chill for at least 3 hours, or overnight. Sift over confectioner's sugar and sprinkle with lemon zest.

PREPARE AHEAD Can be made up to 3 days ahead and kept in the refrigerator.

BAKER'S TIP
If you cannot find any quark it can easily be substituted with low-fat cottage cheese, processed to a paste in a food processor with blade attachment.

CELEBRATION CAKES

Bavarian Raspberry Gâteau

When raspberries are not in season, you can use frozen berries.

SERVES 8	55–60 MINS	20–25 MINS

Chilling time
4 hrs

Special equipment
9in (22cm) springform pan
blender

Ingredients
4 tbsp unsalted butter, plus extra for greasing
1 cup all-purpose flour, plus extra for dusting
pinch of salt
4 large eggs, beaten
⅔ cup sugar
2 tbsp Kirsch

For the raspberry cream
1lb 2oz (500g) raspberries
3 tbsp Kirsch
1 cup sugar
1 cup heavy cream
4 cups milk
1 vanilla bean, split, or 2 tsp pure vanilla extract
10 large egg yolks
3 tbsp cornstarch
1 tbsp unflavored powdered gelatin

Method

1 Preheat the oven to 425°F (220°C). Grease the pan with butter and line the base with buttered parchment paper. Sprinkle in 2–3 tablespoons flour. Melt the butter and let it cool. Sift the flour and salt into a bowl. Put the eggs in a bowl and beat in the sugar, using an electric hand mixer, for 5 minutes.

2 Sift one-third of the flour mixture over the egg mixture and fold in. Add the remaining flour in 2 batches. Fold in the butter. Pour into the pan and bake for 20–25 minutes, until the cake has risen.

3 Turn out the cake onto a wire rack. Let cool. Remove the parchment. Trim the top and bottom so that they are flat. Cut the cake horizontally in half. Clean, dry, and re-grease the pan. Put a cake round in the pan and sprinkle it with 1 tablespoon of the Kirsch.

4 Purée three-quarters of the berries in a blender, then work through a sieve to remove the seeds. Stir in 1 tablespoon of the Kirsch with ½ cup of the sugar. Whip the cream until it forms soft peaks.

5 Put the milk in a pan. Add the vanilla bean, if using. Bring to a boil. Remove the pan from the heat, cover, and let stand in a warm place for 10–15 minutes. Remove the bean. Set aside one-quarter of the milk. Stir the remaining sugar into the milk in the pan.

6 Beat the egg yolks and cornstarch in a bowl. Add the hot milk and whisk until smooth. Pour the yolk mixture back into the pan and cook over medium heat, stirring, until the custard comes to a boil. Stir in the reserved milk and the vanilla extract, if using.

7 Strain the custard equally into 2 bowls. Let cool. Stir 2 tablespoons of Kirsch into one half. Set this custard aside to serve with the finished dessert. Sprinkle the gelatin over 4 tablespoons of water in a small pan and let soften for 5 minutes. Heat until the

gelatin is melted and pourable. Stir into the bowl of unflavored custard, along with the raspberry purée.

8 Set the bowl in a pan of iced water. Stir the mixture until it thickens. Remove the bowl from the water. Fold the raspberry custard into the whipped cream. Pour half into the cake pan. Sprinkle with a few reserved raspberries. Pour the remaining Bavarian cream on the berries. Sprinkle with 1 tablespoon of Kirsch over the second cake round.

9 Lightly press the cake round, sprinkled-side down, on the cream. Cover with plastic wrap and refrigerate for at least 4 hours, until firm. To serve, remove the side of the pan and place on a serving plate. Decorate the top of the cake with the reserved raspberries, and serve the Kirsch custard sauce separately.

PREPARE AHEAD Can be made up to 2 days ahead and kept in the refrigerator; remove 1 hour before serving.

Bienenstich

The name of this German recipe translates as "bee sting" cake. Legend has it that the honey attracts bees that sting the baker!

SERVES 8-10 **20 MINS** **20–25 MINS**

Rising and proofing time
1 hr 5 mins–1 hr 20 mins

Special equipment
8in (20cm) round cake pan

Ingredients
¾ cup all-purpose flour, plus extra for dusting
1 tbsp unsalted butter, softened and diced, plus extra for greasing
2 tsp sugar
1 tsp dried yeast
pinch of salt
1 large egg
oil, for greasing

For the glaze
2 tbsp butter
2 tbsp sugar
1 tbsp honey
1 tbsp heavy cream
⅓ cup (1oz) slivered almonds
1 tsp lemon juice

For the crème pâtissière
1 cup whole milk
1 tbsp cornstarch
2 vanilla beans, split and seeded
¼ cup sugar
3 large egg yolks
2 tbsp unsalted butter, diced

Method

1 Sift the flour into a bowl. Quickly rub in the butter, then add the sugar, yeast, and salt and mix well. Beat in the egg and add enough water to make a soft dough.

2 Knead on a floured surface for 5–10 minutes, or until smooth, elastic, and shiny. Put in a clean, oiled bowl, cover with plastic wrap, and leave to rise in a warm place for 45–60 minutes, or until doubled in size.

3 Grease the cake pan and dust with flour. Knock back the dough and roll it out into a circle, so that it fits the pan. Push it into the pan and cover with plastic wrap. Leave to rise for 20 minutes.

4 To make the glaze, melt the butter in a small pan, then add the sugar, honey, and cream. Cook over low heat until the sugar has dissolved, then increase the heat and bring to a boil. Allow to simmer

for 3 minutes, then remove the pan from the heat and add the almonds and lemon juice. Allow to cool.

5 Preheat the oven to 375°F (190°C). Carefully spread the glaze over the dough, leave to rise for another 10 minutes, then bake for 20–25 minutes, ensuring it doesn't get too dark on the top. Allow to cool in the pan for 30 minutes, then carefully transfer to a wire rack.

6 Now, make the crème pâtissière. Pour the milk into a heavy saucepan and add the cornstarch, vanilla seeds and beans, and half the sugar. Place over low heat. Meanwhile, whisk the egg yolks with the remaining sugar in a bowl. Continue whisking and slowly pour in the hot milk. Transfer to the pan and whisk until it just comes to a boil, then remove from the heat.

7 Immediately place the whole saucepan into a bowl of iced water and remove the vanilla beans. Once the sauce has cooled, add the butter and briskly whisk into the sauce until it is smooth and glossy.

8 Slice the cake in half. Spread a thick layer of crème pâtissière on the bottom half, then place the almond layer on top. Transfer to a serving plate.

BAKER'S TIP

This German recipe is traditionally filled with crème pâtissière, as in this recipe. It makes a smooth, luxurious filling, which, these days, is a real treat. However, if you are pressed for time, an easier option would be to fill the cake with whipped heavy cream, lightly scented with vanilla extract.

Kugelhopf

Dark raisins and chopped almonds are baked into this classic kugelhopf, an Alsatian favorite. A dusting of confectioner's sugar hints at the sweet filling.

| MAKES 1 RING | 45–50 MINS | 45–50 MINS | UP TO 8 WEEKS |

Rising and proofing time
2–2½ hrs

Special equipment
10 cup kugelhopf or ring mold

Ingredients

⅔ cup milk
2 tbsp sugar
11 tbsp unsalted butter, diced,
  plus extra for greasing
1 tbsp dried yeast
3¾ cups bread flour
1 tsp salt
3 large eggs (at room temperature), beaten
½ cup (3oz) raisins
⅓ cup (2oz) blanched almonds, chopped,
  plus 7 whole blanched almonds
confectioner's sugar, for dusting

Method

1 Bring the milk just to a boil in a saucepan, pour ¼ cup of it into a bowl, and let cool to lukewarm. Add the sugar and butter to the milk in the pan and stir until melted. Let cool.

2 Sprinkle the yeast over the ¼ cup milk and let stand for 5 minutes until dissolved, stirring once. Sift the flour and salt into the bowl of an electric mixer fitted with a dough hook. Add the dissolved yeast, eggs, and the butter mixture.

3 Gradually draw in the flour and work it into the other ingredients to form a smooth dough. Knead for 5–7 minutes, until very elastic. It should be very sticky. Cover with a damp kitchen towel and let rise in a warm place for 1–1½ hours, until doubled in bulk.

4 Meanwhile, grease the mold with butter. Freeze the mold until the butter is hard (about 10 minutes) then butter it again. Pour boiling water over the raisins and allow to plump up.

5 Knock back the dough lightly with your hand to push out the air. Drain the raisins, reserving 7 of them, and knead the rest into the dough with the chopped almonds. Arrange the reserved raisins and whole almonds in the bottom of the mold.

6 Drop the dough into the mold, cover with a kitchen towel, and let rise in a warm place until it comes just above the top of the mold. It should take about 30–40 minutes. Preheat the oven to 375°F (190°C) when the bread has risen.

7 Bake the kugelhopf until puffed and brown, and the bread starts to shrink from the side of the mold, 45–50 minutes. Let it cool slightly. Turn out on to a wire rack and let cool completely. Just before serving, sift over the confectioner's sugar.

STORE The kugelhopf will keep in an airtight container for 3 days.

BAKER'S TIP

This dough is very sticky. It is natural to want to add more flour, in order to make it look more like a conventional dough. However, this would be a mistake, as it would make the kugelhopf tough.

Chestnut Millefeuilles

Sure to impress, this dessert is actually quite easy to make and can be prepared up to 6 hours ahead and chilled.

SERVES 8 | **2 HOURS** | **25–30 MINUTES**

Chilling time
1 hr

Ingredients

1½ cups milk
4 large egg yolks
¼ cup sugar
3 tbsp all-purpose flour, sifted
2 tbsp dark rum

1lb 5oz (600g) all-butter puff pastry,
 store-bought
1 cup heavy cream
1lb 2oz (500g) marrons glacés
 (candied chestnuts), crumbled
⅓ cup confectioner's sugar,
 plus extra if needed

CELEBRATION CAKES

1 Heat the milk in a pan over medium heat until it just comes to a boil. Take off heat.

2 Whisk the egg yolks and sugar for 2–3 minutes until thick. Whisk in the flour.

3 Gradually whisk the milk into the egg mixture until smooth. Return to a clean pan.

4 Bring to a boil, whisking, until thickened. Reduce heat to low and whisk for 2 minutes.

5 If lumps form in the pastry cream, remove from the heat and whisk until smooth again.

6 Let cool, then stir in rum. Transfer to a bowl, cover with plastic wrap, and chill for 1 hour.

7 Preheat the oven to 400°F (200°C). Sprinkle a baking sheet evenly with cold water.

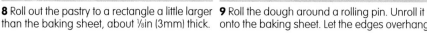

8 Roll out the pastry to a rectangle a little larger than the baking sheet, about ⅛in (3mm) thick.

9 Roll the dough around a rolling pin. Unroll it onto the baking sheet. Let the edges overhang.

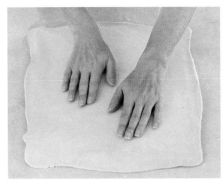

10 Press the dough down lightly on the baking sheet, then chill for about 15 minutes.

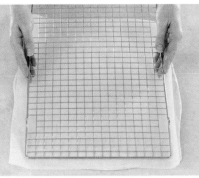

11 Prick the dough all over with a fork. Cover with parchment paper. Set a wire rack on top.

12 Bake for 15–20 minutes. Remove from the oven, grip the sheet and rack, invert the pastry.

13 Slide the baking sheet back under the pastry and bake for another 10 minutes.

14 Remove from the oven and carefully slide the pastry onto a cutting board.

15 While still warm, trim around the edges with a large, sharp knife to neaten.

16 Cut the trimmed sheet lengthwise into 3 equal strips. Allow to cool.

17 Pour the cream into a bowl and whip until fairly firm.

18 Using a large metal spoon, fold the whipped cream into the chilled pastry cream.

19 With a palette knife, spread half the cream mixture evenly over one pastry strip.

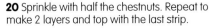

20 Sprinkle with half the chestnuts. Repeat to make 2 layers and top with the last strip.

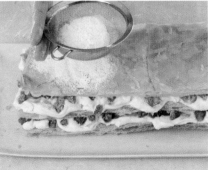

21 Sift over confectioner's sugar and divide into portions with a serrated knife.

Millefeuilles variations

Chocolate Millefeuilles

A decadent and mouth-watering millefeuilles, filled with dark chocolate cream and decorated with white chocolate drizzles.

SERVES 8	2 HOURS	25–30 MINS

Chilling time
1 hr

Ingredients
1 quantity pastry cream, see page 88, steps 1–5
2 tbsp brandy
1lb 5oz (600g) all-butter puff pastry, store-bought
2oz (50g) dark chocolate, melted and cooled
1½ cups heavy cream
1oz (30g) white chocolate, melted and cooled

Method

1 Stir the brandy into the cream, cover with plastic wrap, and chill for 1 hour.

2 Preheat the oven to 400°F (200°C). Sprinkle a baking sheet with cold water. Roll out the pastry to a rectangle larger than the baking sheet. Transfer to the sheet, letting the edges overhang. Press the dough down. Chill for 15 minutes. Prick all over with a fork. Cover with parchment paper, then set a wire rack on top. Bake for 15–20 minutes, until it just begins to brown.

Gripping the sheet and rack, invert the pastry, slide the baking sheet back under and continue baking for 10 minutes, until both sides are browned. Remove from the oven and slide the pastry onto a cutting board. While still warm, trim the edges then cut lengthwise into 3 equal strips. Let cool.

3 Whip the heavy cream until stiff. Stir it into the pastry cream with two-thirds of the melted dark chocolate. Cover and chill. Spread the remaining melted chocolate over one of the pastry strips to cover it. Let it set.

4 Put another pastry strip on a plate, spread with half the cream, top with the remaining strip, and spread with the rest of the cream. Cover with the chocolate-coated strip.

5 Put the white chocolate into one corner of a plastic bag. Twist the bag to enclose the chocolate and snip off the tip of the corner. Pipe trails of chocolate over the millefeuilles.

PREPARE AHEAD The dish can be made ahead and chilled for up to 6 hours.

Vanilla Slices

Classic pastries sandwiched with thick custard and sweet, luscious jam.

MAKES 6	2 HOURS	25–30 MINS

Chilling time
1 hr

Special equipment
small piping bag with thin nozzle

Ingredients
1½ cups heavy cream
1 quantity pastry cream, see page 88, steps 1–5
1lb 5oz (600g) all-butter puff pastry, store-bought
¾ cup confectioner's sugar
1 tsp cocoa powder
½ jar smooth strawberry or raspberry jam

Method

1 Whip the heavy cream until stiff peaks form. Fold it into the pastry cream and chill. Preheat the oven to 400°F (200°C). Sprinkle a baking sheet with cold water. Roll out the pastry to a rectangle larger than the baking sheet, then transfer to the sheet, letting the edges overhang. Press the dough down. Chill for 15 minutes.

2 Prick the dough with a fork. Cover with parchment paper, then set a wire rack on top. Bake for 15–20 minutes, until it just begins to brown. Hold the sheet and rack and invert the pastry. Slide the baking sheet back under and bake for 10 more minutes, until both sides are browned. Remove from the oven and slide the pastry onto a cutting board. While still warm, cut it into 2 x 4in (5 x 10cm) rectangles, in multiples of 3.

3 Put the confectioner's sugar in a bowl and add 1–1½ tablespoons cold water. Take 2 tablespoons out and mix with the cocoa to make a small amount of chocolate icing. Place the chocolate icing in a piping bag with a thin nozzle. Take a third of the pastry pieces and spread them with the white icing. While the icing is wet, pipe horizontal lines across them using the chocolate icing, then drag a skewer through the lines vertically to produce a striped effect. Allow to dry.

4 Spread the remaining pastry pieces with a thin layer of the jam. Spread a ½in (1cm) layer of pastry cream on top of the jam, and clean up the edges with a knife.

5 To assemble the vanilla slices, take a piece of pastry with jam and pastry cream, and place another gently on top. Press down lightly before topping with a third iced piece of pastry.

PREPARE AHEAD The dish can be made ahead and chilled for up to 6 hours.

Summer Fruit Millefeuilles

Beautiful and appetizing on a buffet table, or at a garden tea party. ▶

SERVES 8	2 HOURS	25–30 MINS

Chilling time
1 hr

Ingredients
1 quantity pastry cream, see page 88, steps 1–5
1lb 5oz (600g) all-butter puff pastry, store-bought
1 cup heavy cream
14oz (400g) mixed summer fruits, such as strawberries, diced, and raspberries
confectioner's sugar, for dusting

Method

1 Preheat the oven to 400°F (200°C). Sprinkle a baking sheet evenly with cold water. Roll out the pastry to a rectangle larger than the baking sheet, and about ⅛in (3mm) thick. Roll the dough around a rolling pin, then unroll it onto the baking sheet, letting the edges overhang. Press the dough down. Chill for about 15 minutes.

2 Prick the dough with a fork. Cover with parchment paper, then set a wire rack on top. Bake for 15–20 minutes, until it just begins to brown. Gripping the sheet and rack, invert the pastry. Slide the baking sheet back under and bake for 10 more minutes, until both sides are browned.

Remove from the oven and slide the pastry onto a cutting board. While still warm, trim the edges then cut lengthwise into 3 equal strips. Let cool.

3 Whip the heavy cream until firm. Fold into the pastry cream. Spread half the pastry cream filling over 1 pastry strip. Sprinkle with half the fruit. Repeat with another strip, to make 2 layers. Put the last pastry strip on top, and press down. Sift the confectioner's sugar thickly over the millefeuilles.

PREPARE AHEAD The dish can be made ahead and chilled for up to 6 hours.

BAKER'S TIP
Once you have mastered the art of assembling the pastry, millefeuilles can be made in endless variations. Large, for an impressive buffet centerpiece, or in individual portions for an indulgent afternoon tea, sandwiched together with whatever filling you prefer.

small cakes

Vanilla Cream Cupcakes

A cupcake is quite dense in consistency, which allows it to carry more elaborate types of frosting.

MAKES 24	20 MINS	20–25 MINS	4 WEEKS, UN-ICED

Special equipment
2 x 12-hole cupcake pans
piping bag and star nozzle (optional)

Ingredients
1⅓ cups all-purpose flour
2 tsp baking powder
1 cup sugar
½ tsp salt
7 tbsp unsalted butter, softened
3 large eggs, at room temperature
⅔ cup milk
1 tsp pure vanilla extract

For the frosting
1 cup confectioner's sugar
1 tsp pure vanilla extract
7 tbsp unsalted butter, softened
cupcake sprinkles (optional)

1 Preheat the oven to 350°F (180°C). Place the first 5 ingredients in a bowl.

2 Mix together with your fingertips until it resembles fine bread crumbs.

3 In another bowl, whisk the eggs, milk, and vanilla extract together until well blended.

4 Slowly pour the egg mixture into the dry ingredients, whisking all the time.

5 Whisk gently until smooth, being careful not to over-mix. Too much beating toughens cakes.

6 Pour all the cake batter into a large measuring cup to make it easier to handle.

7 Place the cupcake paper liners into the holes in the cupcake pans.

8 Carefully pour the cake mixture into the liners, filling each one only half full.

9 Bake for around 20 minutes, until lightly colored, firm, and springy to the touch.

SMALL CAKES

10 Check if the cakes are done by inserting a skewer into the center of one cupcake.

11 If traces of cake batter remain on the skewer, cook for a minute more, then test again.

12 Leave for a few minutes, then transfer the cupcakes to a wire rack to cool completely.

13 For the frosting, combine the confectioner's sugar, vanilla extract, and butter in a bowl.

14 Beat with an electric hand mixer until very light and fluffy; this will take about 5 minutes.

15 To be sure the cakes are completely cool to the touch, or they will begin to melt the frosting.

16 If frosting by hand, add a spoonful of the frosting mix to the top of each cake.

17 Then use the back of a spoon dipped in warm water to smooth the surface.

18 For a more professional result, transfer the frosting to the piping bag.

19 Pipe by squeezing out the frosting with one hand while holding the cake with the other.

20 Starting from the edge, pipe a spiral of frosting that comes to a peak in the center.

21 Decorate with sprinkles. **STORE** Will keep in an airtight container for 3 days.

VANILLA CREAM CUPCAKES

Cupcake variations

Chocolate Cupcakes

Classic chocolate cupcakes are another must-have recipe. A guaranteed winner for children's parties!

MAKES 24	20 MINS	20–25 MINS	4 WEEKS, UN-ICED

Special equipment
2 x 12-hole cupcake pans
piping bag and star nozzle (optional)

Ingredients
1⅓ cups all-purpose flour
2 tsp baking powder
4 tbsp cocoa powder
1 cup sugar
½ tsp salt
7 tbsp unsalted butter, softened
3 large eggs, at room temperature
⅔ cup milk
1 tsp pure vanilla extract
1 tbsp Greek yogurt

For the frosting
1 cup confectioner's sugar
¼ cup cocoa powder
7 tbsp softened butter

Method

1 Preheat the oven to 350°F (180°C). Sift the flour, baking powder, and cocoa into a bowl. Add the sugar, salt, and butter. Mix until it resembles fine bread crumbs. In a bowl, whisk the eggs, milk, vanilla extract, and yogurt together until well blended.

2 Slowly pour in the egg mixture to combine. Mix gently until smooth. Place the cupcake paper liners into the holes in the cupcake pans. Spoon the mixture into the liners, filling each one only half full.

3 Bake for around 20 minutes, until lightly colored, firm, and springy to the touch. Leave for a few minutes, then transfer the cupcakes to a wire rack to cool completely.

4 For the frosting, beat the confectioner's sugar, cocoa powder, and butter until smooth.

5 Frost by hand, using the back of a spoon dipped in warm water to smooth the surface, or transfer the frosting to the piping bag and pipe on to the cakes.

STORE These cupcakes keep in an airtight container for 3 days.

Lemon Cupcakes

For a delicate taste, try flavoring the basic cupcake batter with lemon.

MAKES 24	20 MINS	20–25 MINS	4 WEEKS, UN-ICED

Special equipment
2 x 12-hole cupcake pans
piping bag and star nozzle (optional)

Ingredients
1⅓ cups all-purpose flour
2 tsp baking powder
1 cup sugar
½ tsp salt
7 tbsp unsalted butter, softened
3 large eggs, at room temperature
⅔ cup milk
finely grated zest and juice of 1 lemon

For the frosting
7 tbsp unsalted butter, softened
1 cup confectioner's sugar

Method

1 Preheat the oven to 350°F (180°C). Sift the flour and baking powder into a bowl. Add the sugar, salt, and butter. Mix until it resembles fine bread crumbs. In a bowl, whisk the eggs and milk until well blended.

2 Pour in the egg mixture to combine. Add half the lemon zest and all the lemon juice. Mix gently until smooth. Place the cupcake paper liners into the cupcake pans. Spoon the mixture into the papers, filling each one only half full. Bake for 20–25 minutes, until springy. Cool completely on a wire rack.

3 To make the frosting, beat the butter, confectioner's sugar, and remaining lemon zest until smooth. Frost by hand, using the back of a spoon, or with the piping bag.

STORE These cupcakes keep in an airtight container for 3 days.

BAKER'S TIP
Due to their fairly dense texture, these classic cupcakes will keep well for a few days. If you prefer them well risen, replace the all-purpose flour with self-rising flour but reduce the baking powder to 1 teaspoon, accordingly.

Coffee and Walnut Cupcakes

Definitely one for adults, coffee and nuts add depth to these cupcakes.

MAKES 24 | 20 MINS | 20–25 MINS | 4 WEEKS, UN-ICED

Special equipment
2 x 12-hole cupcake pans
piping bag and star nozzle (optional)

Ingredients
1⅓ cups all-purpose flour, plus more for dusting
2 tsp baking powder
1 cup sugar
½ tsp salt
7 tbsp unsalted butter, softened
3 large eggs, at room temperature
⅔ cup milk
1 tbsp instant coffee and 1 tbsp boiling water, combined and cooled, or 1 cooled espresso
1 cup halved walnuts, plus extra

For the frosting
7 tbsp unsalted butter, softened
1 cup confectioner's sugar
1 tsp pure vanilla extract

Method

1 Preheat the oven to 350°F (180°C). Sift the flour and baking powder into a bowl. Add the sugar, salt, and butter. Mix until it resembles fine bread crumbs. In a bowl, whisk the eggs and milk until well blended.

2 Pour in the egg mixture, add half the coffee, and mix until smooth. Coarsely chop the walnuts and toss them in a bowl with a little flour, then fold them into the batter. Place the cupcake liners in the trays. Spoon the mixture into the liners, filling each one only half full. Bake for 20–25 minutes until springy, then cool completely on a wire rack.

3 To make the frosting, beat the butter, confectioner's sugar, vanilla extract, and remaining coffee until smooth. Frost by hand, with the back of a spoon, or with the piping bag. Top each cake with a walnut half.

STORE These cupcakes keep in an airtight container for 3 days.

Fondant Fancies

Dainty in size, gorgeous to look at, and delectable to eat, these little cakes are perfect for a party or as a special afternoon treat.

MAKES 16 | 20–25 MINS | 25 MINS

Special equipment
8in (20cm) square cake pan

Ingredients
12 tbsp unsalted butter, plus extra for greasing
1⅓ cups all-purpose flour, plus extra for dusting
1½ tsp baking powder
½ tsp salt
¾ cup sugar

3 large eggs, at room temperature
1 tsp pure vanilla extract
2 tbsp milk
2–3 tbsp raspberry or red cherry conserve

For the buttercream
5 tbsp unsalted butter, at room temperature
¾ cup confectioner's sugar

For the frosting
juice of ½ lemon
3⅔ cups confectioner's sugar
1–2 drops natural pink food coloring
icing flowers, to decorate (optional)

Method

1 Preheat the oven to 375°F (190°C). Grease the cake pan and dust with flour. Sift flour, baking powder, and salt into a bowl. Place the butter and sugar in a large bowl, or the bowl of an electric mixer, and beat until pale and fluffy. Set aside.

2 Lightly beat the eggs and vanilla extract in another large bowl. Add about ¼ of the egg mixture and 1 tablespoon of the flour mixture to the butter mixture and beat well, then add the rest of the egg, a little at a time, beating as you go. Add the rest of the flour mixture and the milk, and mix in gently.

3 Transfer the mixture to the prepared pan and bake in the middle of the oven for about 25 minutes, or until lightly golden and springy to the touch. Remove from the oven, leave to cool in the pan for about 10 minutes, then remove from the pan and cool upside down on a wire rack.

4 To make the buttercream, beat the butter with the confectioner's sugar until smooth. Set aside. Slice the cake horizontally and

spread the fruit conserve on one half and the buttercream on the other. Sandwich together, then cut into 16 equal squares.

5 To make the frosting, put the lemon juice in a measuring cup and fill it up to a ¼ cup with hot water. Mix this with the confectioner's sugar, stirring continuously and adding more hot water as required until the mixture is smooth. Add the pink food coloring and stir well.

6 Use a palette knife to transfer the cakes to a wire rack placed over a board or plate (to catch the drips), then drizzle with the icing to cover the cakes completely, or just cover the tops of the cakes and allow the icing to drip down the sides so the sponge layers are visible. Decorate with icing flowers (if using), then leave to set for about 15 minutes. Use a clean palette knife to transfer each cake carefully to a paper liner.

STORE These fancies will keep in the refrigerator for 1 day.

BAKER'S TIP
These little fancies are beautiful, but for a chocolate version, chill the filled squares well, then pierce each with a cocktail stick. Holding the stick, dip each cake into a bowl of dark melted chocolate, then set on a wire rack. Once set, drizzle with melted white chocolate for a contrasting pattern.

Chocolate Fudge Cake Balls

These are the new "it" cakes. Deceptively simple to make, packaged or leftover cake can also be used.

MAKES 20–25 | **35 MINS** | **25 MINS** | **4 WEEKS, UNDIPPED**

Chilling time
3 hours, or 30 mins freezing

Special equipment
8in (20cm) cake pan

Ingredients
7 tbsp unsalted butter, softened, or soft margarine, plus extra for greasing
½ cup sugar
2 large eggs, at room temperature
⅔ cup all-purpose flour
¼ cup cocoa powder, plus extra for dusting
1 tsp baking powder
¼ tsp salt
5 tbsp milk, plus extra if needed
½ cup (6oz) store-bought chocolate fudge frosting (or use recipe for Chocolate Fudge Cake frosting, page 46)
10oz (250g) chocolate coating bark
2oz (50g) white chocolate

1 Preheat the oven to 350°F (180°C). Grease the pan and line with parchment paper.

2 With an electric hand mixer, cream the butter and sugar until fluffy.

3 Beat in the eggs one at a time, beating well in between each, until smooth and creamy.

4 Sift together the flour, cocoa, baking powder, and salt and mix into the cake batter.

5 Mix in enough milk to loosen the batter to a dropping consistency.

6 Pour into the pan and bake for 25 minutes, until the top is springy to the touch.

7 Check the cake is cooked; a skewer inserted should emerge clean. Turn on to a wire rack.

8 When the cake is cool, process it in a food processor until it resembles bread crumbs.

9 Add the frosting and blend together to a smooth, uniform color.

SMALL CAKES

10 Using dry hands, roll the cake mix into balls, each the size of a walnut.

11 Put the balls on a plate and refrigerate for 3 hours or freeze for 30 minutes until quite firm.

12 Line 2 baking sheets with parchment paper. Melt the chocolate coating bark.

13 Take a few cake balls at a time. Put them, one by one, into the molten chocolate mixture.

14 Using 2 forks, turn the balls in the chocolate until covered. Remove, allowing excess to drip.

15 Transfer the coated cake balls to the baking sheets to dry. Continue to coat all the cakes.

16 Melt the white chocolate in a bowl over a saucepan of simmering water.

17 Drizzle the white chocolate over the cakes with a spoon, to decorate.

18 Leave the white chocolate to dry completely before transferring to a serving plate.
STORE The cakes can be kept in an airtight container for 3 days.

Cake Ball variations

Strawberries and Cream Cake Pops

These are a fantastically impressive treat to serve at a children's party. You could even decorate a whole birthday cake with them.

| MAKES 20–25 | 20 MINS | 25 MINS | 4 WEEKS, UNDIPPED |

Chilling time
3 hrs, or 30 mins freezing

Special equipment
8in (20cm) round cake pan
food processor
25 pieces of bamboo skewer, cut to
approximately 4in (10cm) lengths,
to resemble lollipop sticks

Ingredients
7 tbsp unsalted butter, softened, plus extra
¾ cup all-purpose flour, plus extra for dusting
½ cup sugar
2 large eggs, at room temperature
1 tsp baking powder
¼ tsp salt
½ cup store-bought buttercream frosting, (or see
vanilla buttercream frosting, page 109)
2 tbsp good quality, smooth strawberry jam
10oz (300g) white chocolate coating bark

Method
1 Preheat the oven to 350°F (180°C). Grease the cake pan and dust with flour. Cream together the butter and sugar. Beat in the eggs one at a time, until the mixture is smooth and creamy. Sift together the flour, baking powder, and salt and mix into the cake batter.

2 Pour the batter into the pan and bake for 20–30 minutes, until the surface is springy to the touch. Turn out to cool on a wire rack.

3 When the cake is cool, process it until it resembles bread crumbs. Weigh out 2¾ cups and place in a bowl. Add the frosting and the jam and mix thoroughly. Using dry hands, roll the mix into balls the size of a walnut. Put the balls on a plate and stick a skewer into each. Refrigerate for 3 hours or freeze for 30 minutes. Line a baking sheet with parchment paper.

4 Melt the coating bark in a bowl set over barely simmering water. Dip the chilled balls one at a time into the molten chocolate, turning until completely covered, right up to the stick.

5 Gently take them out of the chocolate mixture and allow any excess to drip back into the bowl before transferring them to the baking sheets to dry. The pops should be eaten on the same day.

> **BAKER'S TIP**
> To ensure a smooth, round finish to cake pops, cut an apple in half and place the halves cut side down on the lined baking sheet. Dip the cake pops, then stick their bamboo skewers into the apple. This will help the cake pops dry without any marks on the surface.

Fruit Cake Balls

I love to serve these cute little cakes at Christmas parties. An easy and delicious way to use up leftover fruit cake.

| MAKES 15–20 | 20 MINS | 25 MINS | 4 WEEKS, UNDIPPED |

Chilling time
3 hrs, or 30 mins freezing

Special equipment
food processor

Ingredients
2 cups leftover Fruit Cake (see recipe, page 72)
6oz (150g) dark chocolate coating bark
2oz (50g) white chocolate coating bark
glacé cherries and candied angelica (optional)

Method
1 Pulse the cold fruit cake in a food processor until thoroughly broken up. Using dry hands, roll the fruit cake into balls about the size of a walnut. Put the balls on a plate and refrigerate them for 3 hours or freeze for 30 minutes until quite firm.

2 Line 2 baking sheets with wax paper. In a small, microwave-proof bowl, heat the dark chocolate coating bark in bursts of 30 seconds until it is melted, but not too hot. Or, melt it in a small heatproof bowl over a saucepan of barely simmering water.

3 Take the cake balls out of the refrigerator a few at a time. Dip them, one at a time, into the molten chocolate mixture, turning them quickly with 2 forks until covered in chocolate. Take them out of the chocolate mixture and allow any excess chocolate to drip back into the bowl. Transfer them to the lined baking sheets to dry. Continue the process until all of the balls are coated. You will have to work quickly, as the chocolate can harden very fast, and the cake balls can disintegrate if left in the warm chocolate for too long.

4 Melt the white chocolate coating bark as above. Using a teaspoon, drop a little of the white chocolate mixture on to the top of the hardened fruit cake balls, so that it looks as if they have been drizzled with icing, or snow. The white chocolate should drip down the sides a little bit.

5 If you are feeling ambitious, small slivers of glacé cherries and candied angelica can be cut to resemble holly leaves and berries and stuck to the still molten white chocolate. Leave the cake balls to rest until the white chocolate is quite hard.

STORE Will keep in the refrigerator for 5 days.

White Chocolate and Coconut Snowballs

These coconut balls are sophisticated enough to serve as canapés.

| MAKES 25–30 | 40 MINS | 25 MINS | 4 WEEKS, UNDIPPED |

Chilling time
3 hrs, or 30 mins freezing

Special equipment
8in (20cm) cake pan
food processor

Ingredients
7 tbsp unsalted butter, softened, plus extra for greasing
½ cup sugar
2 large eggs, at room temperature
1 cup all-purpose flour, plus more for dusting
1 tsp baking powder
1¼ cups store-bought buttercream frosting, (or see vanilla buttercream frosting, page 109)
8oz (225g) unsweetened, shredded coconut
10oz (300g) white chocolate coating bark

Method

1 Preheat the oven to 350°F (180°C). Grease the pan and line the base with parchment paper. Cream the butter and sugar until pale and fluffy. Beat in the eggs one at a time, beating well between each addition. Sift together the flour and baking powder, and mix into the cake batter.

2 Pour the batter into the pan and bake for 25 minutes. Turn out to cool on a wire rack. Remove the baking parchment.

3 When the cake is cool, process until it resembles fine bread crumbs. Weigh out 2¾ cups of the crumbs and put them in a bowl. Add the frosting and 3oz (75g) of the coconut and cream the mixture together

4 Using dry hands, roll the mix into balls the size of a walnut. Refrigerate for 3 hours or freeze for 30 minutes. Line a baking sheet with parchment paper and put the remaining coconut on a plate.

5 Melt the coating bark in a heatproof bowl over a saucepan of barely simmering water. Place the chilled cake balls, one at a time, into the melted chocolate mixture, using two forks to turn them until covered.

6 Transfer them to the plate of coconut. Roll them around in the coconut, then transfer to the baking sheet to dry. You will have to work fast, as the chocolate can harden quickly, and the balls start to disintegrate if they are left in the chocolate too long.

STORE The cake balls will keep in a cool place in an airtight container for 2 days.

Whoopie Pies

Fast becoming a modern classic, whoopie pies are a quick and easy way to please a crowd.

MAKES 10 PIES | **40 MINS** | **12 MINS** | **4 WEEKS, UNFILLED**

Ingredients
12 tbsp unsalted butter, softened
¾ cup light brown sugar
1 large egg, at room temperature
1 tsp pure vanilla extract
1¾ cups all-purpose flour
⅔ cup cocoa powder
2 tsp baking powder
1 tsp salt

⅔ cup whole milk
2 tbsp Greek yogurt

For the vanilla buttercream
7 tbsp unsalted butter, softened
1 cup confectioner's sugar
2 tsp pure vanilla extract
2 tsp milk, plus extra if necessary

To decorate
white and dark chocolate
7oz (200g) confectioner's sugar

1 Preheat the oven to 350°F (180°C). Line several baking sheets with parchment paper.

2 With an electric hand mixer, cream together the butter and sugar until light and fluffy.

3 Add the egg and vanilla extract to the creamed mixture and beat in.

4 Beat the egg in well to avoid curdling. The cake batter should look as shown above.

5 In a separate large bowl, sift together the flour, cocoa powder, baking powder, and salt.

6 Gently fold a spoonful of the dry ingredients into the cake batter.

7 Add a little of the milk and gently mix in. Repeat until everything is combined.

8 Blend in the yogurt, folding gently, until very well combined; this will moisten the pies.

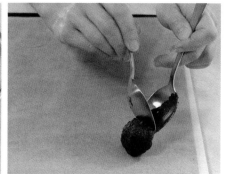

9 Place 20 heaping tablespoons of mixture on the lined baking sheets.

SMALL CAKES

10 Leave space for the mixture to spread out; each half will spread to 3in (8cm).

11 Dip a clean tablespoon in warm water and use it to smooth the surface of the balls.

12 Bake for around 12 minutes, until a skewer comes out clean. Cool on a wire rack.

13 Mix together the buttercream ingredients, except the milk, with a wooden spoon initially.

14 Add the milk, change to a mixer, and beat the mix for 5 minutes, until light and fluffy.

15 If the mixture seems stiff, loosen with extra milk to make the buttercream spreadable.

16 Spread a tablespoon of the buttercream onto the flat sides of half the cakes.

17 Sandwich together the iced with the un-iced halves to form the pies, pressing gently.

18 To decorate, use a vegetable peeler to produce white and dark chocolate shavings.

19 Place the confectioner's sugar in a bowl and add water to form a thick paste.

20 Spoon the frosting onto the top each pie, spreading it out for an even covering.

21 Lightly press the chocolate shavings onto the wet icing. **STORE** Will keep for 2 days.

Whoopie Pie variations

Peanut Butter Whoopie Pies

Sweet, salty, and creamy, these whoopie pies are addictive.

MAKES 20 PIES — **40 MINS** — **12 MINS** — **4 WEEKS, UNFILLED**

Ingredients
12 tbsp unsalted butter, softened
¾ cup light brown sugar
1 large egg, at room temperature
1 tsp pure vanilla extract
2 cups all-purpose flour
⅔ cup cocoa powder
2 tsp baking powder
1 tsp salt
⅔ cup whole milk
2 tbsp Greek yogurt or thick plain yogurt
2oz (60g) cream cheese, at room temperature
¼ cup smooth peanut butter
1 cup confectioner's sugar, sifted
2 tsp milk, plus extra if necessary

Method
1 Preheat the oven to 350°F (180°C). Line several baking sheets with parchment paper. Place the butter and sugar into the bowl of an electric mixer. Cream together until fluffy. Beat in the egg and vanilla.

2 In a separate bowl, sift the flour, cocoa powder, baking powder, and salt. Mix the dry ingredients and milk into the batter by turns, a spoonful at a time. Fold in the yogurt.

3 Put heaping tablespoons of the batter on the baking sheets, leaving space for the mixture to spread. Roll into smooth balls with wet hands, then press down gently. Bake for 12 minutes. Turn out on a wire rack.

4 Beat together the cream cheese and peanut butter until smooth. Cream in the confectioner's sugar, adding a little milk if needed. Spread the frosting on to the flat sides of half the cakes. Sandwich together with the un-iced cakes to make the pies.

STORE The whoopie pies will keep in the refrigerator for 1 day.

Chocolate Orange Whoopie Pies

Rich, dark chocolate combined with the zesty tang of orange is a classic combination, used here to full advantage in these delicious little cakes.

MAKES 20 PIES — **40 MINS** — **12 MINS** — **4 WEEKS, UNFILLED**

Ingredients
18 tbsp unsalted butter, softened
¾ cup light brown sugar
1 large egg
2 tsp pure vanilla extract
finely grated zest and juice of 1 orange
1½ cups all-purpose flour
⅔ cup cocoa powder
½ tsp baking powder
½ tsp salt
⅔ cup whole milk or buttermilk
2 tbsp Greek yogurt or thick plain yogurt
1⅔ cups confectioner's sugar

Method
1 Preheat the oven to 350°F (180°C). Line several baking sheets with parchment paper. Cream 12 tablespoons butter and the brown sugar. Beat in the egg and 1 teaspoon vanilla and add the zest. In a bowl sift the flour, cocoa, baking powder, and salt. Mix the dry ingredients and the milk into the batter, in alternate spoonfuls. Fold in the yogurt.

2 Place heaping tablespoons onto the baking sheets, leaving space between them. Roll into smooth balls with wet hands, then press down gently onto the baking sheets. Bake for 12 minutes, until risen. Leave to cool slightly, then transfer to a wire rack.

3 For the frosting, blend the remaining butter, confectioner's sugar, 1 teaspoon vanilla, and orange juice, loosening with a little water. Spread 1 tablespoon of the filling onto the flat side of each cake half and sandwich together with the remaining halves.

STORE The whoopie pies will keep for 2 days.

Coconut Whoopie Pies

This simple yet delicious variation uses the natural affinity between coconut and chocolate to great effect.

MAKES 20 PIES — **40 MINS** — **12 MINS** — **4 WEEKS, UNFILLED**

Ingredients
12 tbsp unsalted butter, softened
¾ cup light brown sugar
1 large egg, at room temperature
1 tsp pure vanilla extract
2 cups all-purpose flour
⅔ cup cocoa powder
2 tsp baking powder
1 tsp salt
⅔ cup whole milk
2 tbsp Greek yogurt or thick plain yogurt

For the coconut frosting
7 tbsp unsalted butter, softened
1 cup confectioner's sugar
1 tsp pure vanilla extract
2 tsp whole milk
5 tbsp unsweetened, flaked coconut

Method
1 Preheat the oven to 350°F (180°C). Line several baking sheets with parchment paper. Cream together the butter and sugar until fluffy. Beat in the egg and vanilla. In a separate bowl, sift together the flour, cocoa powder, baking powder, and salt. Mix the dry ingredients and the milk into the batter by turns, a spoonful at a time. Fold in the yogurt.

2 Put tablespoons of batter onto the sheets. Roll into smooth balls with wet hands, then press down gently onto the baking sheets. Bake for 12 minutes, until risen. Leave to cool slightly, then transfer to a wire rack. Soak the coconut for 10 minutes in a little milk. Drain.

3 For the frosting, whisk the butter, confectioner's sugar, vanilla, and milk until fluffy. Beat in the coconut. Spread on half the cakes. Sandwich with the remaining halves.

Black Forest Whoopie Pies

A modern imitation of the famous gâteau, using canned cherries.

MAKES 20 PIES · **40 MINS** · **12 MINS** · **4 WEEKS, UNFILLED**

Ingredients
12 tbsp unsalted butter, softened
¾ cup light brown sugar
1 large egg
1 tsp pure vanilla extract
1½ cups all-purpose flour
⅔ cup cocoa powder
½ tsp baking powder
½ tsp salt
⅔ cup whole milk or buttermilk
2 tbsp Greek yogurt or thick plain yogurt
8oz (225g) canned black cherries, drained, or use frozen, defrosted
9oz (250g) mascarpone
2 tbsp sugar

Method
1 Preheat the oven to 350°F (180°C). Line several baking sheets with parchment paper. Cream the butter and brown sugar until fluffy. Beat in the egg and vanilla.

2 In a bowl, sift the flour, cocoa, baking powder, and salt. Mix the dry ingredients and the milk into the batter, in alternate spoonfuls. Fold in the yogurt. Chop 4oz (100g) of the cherries and fold these in, too.

3 Place heaping tablespoons onto the baking sheets, leaving space between them. Roll into smooth balls with wet hands, then press down gently onto the baking sheets. Bake for 12 minutes. Transfer to a wire rack.

4 Purée the remaining cherries until smooth. Mix the blended cherries and sugar into the mascarpone until well mixed; alternatively, leave a ripple effect in the filling. Spread 1 tablespoon of the filling onto the flat side of each cooled cake half, and sandwich together with the remaining halves.

STORE Best eaten the day of baking but can be stored for 1 day in the refrigerator.

Strawberries and Cream Whoopie Pies

Best served immediately, these strawberry layered whoopie pies make a lovely addition to a traditional afternoon tea.

MAKES 20 PIES · **40 MINS** · **12 MINS** · **4 WEEKS, UNFILLED**

Ingredients
12 tbsp unsalted butter, softened
¾ cup light brown sugar
1 large egg, at room temperature
1 tsp pure vanilla extract
1¾ cups all-purpose flour
½ cup cocoa powder
2 tsp baking powder
1 tsp salt
⅔ cup whole milk
2 tbsp Greek yogurt or thick plain yogurt
⅔ cup heavy cream, whipped
9oz (250g) strawberries, sliced
confectioner's sugar, for dusting

Method
1 Preheat the oven to 350°F (180°C). Line several baking sheets with parchment paper.

Cream together the butter and sugar until fluffy. Beat in the egg and vanilla. In a separate bowl, sift together the flour, cocoa powder, baking powder, and salt. Mix the dry ingredients and the milk into the batter by turns, a spoonful at a time. Fold in the yogurt.

2 Put heaping tablespoons of the batter onto the baking sheets, leaving space for the mixture to spread. Roll into smooth balls with wet hands, then press down gently onto the baking sheets.

3 Bake for 12 minutes, until well risen. Leave the pies for a few minutes, then turn out to cool completely on a wire rack.

4 Spread the whipped cream on half the cakes. Top with a layer of sliced strawberries and a second cake. Dust with confectioner's sugar and serve immediately.

Chocolate Fondants

Usually thought of as a restaurant dessert, chocolate fondants are really surprisingly easy to prepare at home.

SERVES 4 | 20 MINS | 5–15 MINS | 1 WEEK, UNBAKED

Special equipment
4 x 5fl oz (150ml) dariole molds
 or 4in (10cm) ramekins

Ingredients
11 tbsp unsalted butter, cubed,
 plus extra for greasing

1 heaping tbsp all-purpose flour,
 plus extra for sprinkling
6oz (150g) good-quality dark chocolate,
 minimum 60% cocoa solids
3 large eggs, at room temperature
⅓ cup sugar
cocoa powder or confectioner's sugar, for dusting
ice cream, to serve

Method

1 Preheat the oven to 400°F (200°C). Thoroughly grease the ramekins with butter and sprinkle with a little flour, then turn it around in the dish until the butter is covered with a thin layer of flour. Tap out the excess.

2 Line the bases of the ramekins with small disks of parchment paper. In a heatproof bowl over simmering water, gently melt together the chocolate and butter, stirring all the time. Make sure the base of the bowl does not touch the water. Cool slightly.

3 In a separate bowl, whisk together the eggs and sugar. Once the chocolate mixture has cooled slightly, beat it into the eggs and sugar until thoroughly amalgamated. Sift the flour over the top and blend it in.

4 Divide the mixture between the molds or ramekins, making sure that the mixture does not come right up to the top. At this stage the fondants can be refrigerated for up to 12 hours, as long as they are brought back to room temperature before cooking.

5 Cook the fondants in the middle of the oven for 5–6 minutes if using molds, 12–15 minutes for ramekins. The sides should be firm, but the middles soft to the touch. Run a sharp knife around the edge of the molds or ramekins. Turn the fondants out on to individual serving plates by placing a plate on top and inverting the whole thing. Gently remove the mold or ramekin and peel off the parchment paper.

6 Dust with cocoa powder or confectioner's sugar if desired and serve immediately with ice cream. The middle should be completely liquid.

PREPARE AHEAD The uncooked mixture in the molds or ramekins can be refrigerated overnight (see Baker's Tip).

BAKER'S TIP
Chocolate fondants are surprisingly simple to get right. They can be prepared up to a day in advance, which makes them a great dinner party dessert. Bring them back to room temperature before they go into the oven (and do the same after defrosting), or they may need to be cooked for slightly longer.

Lemon and Blueberry Muffins

These featherlight muffins are glazed with lemon juice for an extra burst of flavor. Best served warm.

MAKES 12 **20–25 MINS** **15–20 MINS** **UP TO 4 WEEKS**

Special equipment
12-hole muffin pan

Ingredients
4 tbsp unsalted butter
2 cups all-purpose flour
1 tbsp baking powder
½ tsp salt
½ cup sugar
1 large egg, at room temperature

finely grated zest and juice of
  1 lemon
1 tsp pure vanilla extract
1 cup milk
2¼ cups blueberries

1 Preheat the oven to 425°F (220°C). Melt the butter in a saucepan over medium-low heat.

2 Sift the flour, baking powder, and salt into a bowl (do not make muffins in an electric mixer).

3 Set 2 tablespoons sugar aside and stir the rest into the flour. Make a well in the center.

4 In a separate bowl, beat the egg lightly until just broken down and mixed together.

5 Add the melted butter, lemon zest, vanilla, and milk. Beat the egg mixture until foamy.

6 In a slow, steady stream, pour the egg mixture into the well in the flour.

7 Stir with a rubber spatula, gradually drawing in the dry ingredients to make a smooth batter.

8 Gently fold in all the blueberries, being sure not to bruise any of the fruits.

9 Do not over-mix, or the muffins will be tough. Stop when the ingredients are blended.

10 Place the muffin liners in the pan. Spoon in the batter, filling to three-quarters full.

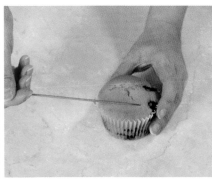

11 Bake for 15–20 minutes, until a skewer inserted in the center comes out clean.

12 Let the muffins cool slightly, then transfer them to a wire rack.

13 In a small bowl, stir the reserved sugar with the lemon juice until the sugar dissolves.

14 While the muffins are warm, dip the crown of each into the sugar and lemon mixture.

15 Set the muffins upright back on the wire rack and brush with any remaining glaze.

16 The warm muffins will absorb the maximum amount of the lemony glaze.
STORE Best served warm, but will keep in an airtight container for 2 days.

Muffin variations

Chocolate Muffins

These muffins will fix chocolate cravings, and the buttermilk lends a delicious lightness.

MAKES 12	10 MINS	15 MINS	UP TO 8 WEEKS

Special equipment
12-hole muffin pan

Ingredients
1¾ cups all-purpose flour
⅔ cup cocoa powder
1 tbsp baking powder
pinch of salt
½ cup light brown sugar
¾ cup chocolate chips
1 cup buttermilk
6 tbsp sunflower oil
½ tsp pure vanilla extract
2 large eggs, at room temperature

Method
1 Preheat the oven to 400°F (200°C). Line the muffin pan with paper muffin liners and set aside. Sift the flour, cocoa powder, baking powder, and salt into a large bowl. Stir in the sugar and chocolate chips, then make a well in the center of the dry ingredients.

2 Beat together the buttermilk, oil, vanilla, and eggs and pour the mixture into the center of the dry ingredients. Mix together lightly to make a lumpy batter. Spoon the mixture into the paper liners, filling each ¾ of the way full.

3 Bake for 15 minutes, or until well risen and firm to the touch. Immediately transfer the muffins to a wire rack and leave to cool.

STORE The muffins will keep in an airtight container for 2 days.

BAKER'S TIP
The use of liquid in these muffins, whether sour cream, buttermilk, or oil, will ensure a moist, longer lasting cake. If a recipe calls for oil, make sure that you use a light, flavorless one such as sunflower or vegetable to ensure that the delicious flavors of the muffins are not masked by the taste of the oil.

Lemon Poppy-seed Muffins

The poppy seeds add a pleasing crunch to these delicate muffins.

MAKES 12	20–25 MINS	15–20 MINS	UP TO 4 WEEKS

Special equipment
12-hole muffin pan

Ingredients
4 tbsp unsalted butter
1¾ cups all-purpose flour
1 tbsp baking powder
½ tsp salt
½ cup sugar, plus 2 tsp for sprinkling
1 large egg, at room temperature, beaten
1 tsp pure vanilla extract
1 cup milk
2 tbsp poppy seeds
finely grated zest and juice of 1 lemon

Method
1 Preheat the oven to 425°F (220°C). Melt the butter in a saucepan over medium-low heat, then leave to cool slightly. Sift the flour, baking powder, and salt into a large bowl (do not make muffins in an electric mixer). Stir in the sugar. Make a well in the center of the dry ingredients.

2 Put the egg in a separate bowl; add the melted butter, vanilla, and milk. Beat the egg mixture until foamy. Stir in the poppy seeds and the lemon zest and juice.

3 In a slow, steady stream, pour the egg mixture into the well in the flour. Stir to make a smooth batter, but do not over-mix, or the muffins will be tough. Stop as soon as the ingredients are blended.

4 Place the muffin liners in the muffin pan. Spoon the batter evenly between the liners. Sprinkle evenly with 2 teaspoons of sugar.

5 Bake for 15–20 minutes. Let the muffins cool slightly, then transfer them to a wire rack to cool completely.

STORE The muffins will keep in an airtight container for 2 days.

Apple Muffins

These healthier muffins are best served straight from the oven.

MAKES 12 **10 MINS** **20–25 MINS** **UP TO 8 WEEKS**

Special equipment
12-hole muffin pan

Ingredients
1 Golden Delicious apple, peeled and chopped
2 tsp lemon juice
½ cup light brown sugar, plus extra for sprinkling
1½ cups all-purpose flour
⅔ cup whole wheat flour
4 tsp baking powder
1 tbsp ground pumpkin pie spice
½ tsp salt
⅓ cup (2oz) pecans, chopped
1 cup milk
¼ cup sunflower oil
1 large egg, at room temperature, beaten

Method
1 Preheat the oven to 400°F (200°C). Line the muffin pan with the paper liners and set aside. Put the apple in a bowl, add the lemon juice, and toss. Add 4 tbsp of the sugar and set aside for 5 minutes.

2 Meanwhile, sift both flours, baking powder, pumpkin pie spice, and salt into a large bowl, adding in any bran left in the sieve. Stir in the remaining sugar and pecans, then make a well in the center of the dry ingredients.

3 Beat together the milk, oil, and egg, then add the apple. Pour the wet ingredients into the center of the dry ingredients and mix together lightly to make a lumpy batter.

4 Spoon the mixture into the paper liners, filling each liner ¾ of the way full. Bake the muffins for 20–25 minutes, or until the tops are peaked and brown. Transfer the muffins to a wire rack and sprinkle with extra sugar. Eat warm or cooled.

STORE The muffins will keep in an airtight container for 2 days.

MUFFIN VARIATIONS

Madeleines

These elegant treats were made famous by French writer Marcel Proust, who took a bite and was transported back to his childhood.

MAKES 12 | 15–20 MINS | 10 MINS | UP TO 4 WEEKS

Special equipment
Madeleine pan, or 12-hole mini muffin pan

Ingredients
4 tbsp unsalted butter, melted and cooled
⅓ cup all-purpose flour, sifted, plus extra for dusting
⅓ cup sugar
2 large eggs, at room temperature
1 tsp pure vanilla extract
¼ tsp baking powder
confectioner's sugar, to dust

Method

1 Preheat the oven to 350°F (180°C). Liberally brush the pan with melted butter and dust with flour. Invert the pan and tap to remove excess flour.

2 Put the sugar, eggs, and vanilla into a mixing bowl and whisk until the mixture is pale, thick, and will hold a trail. This should take 5 minutes with an electric hand mixer, or a bit longer if you are whisking by hand.

3 Sift the flour over the top and pour the melted butter down the side of the mixture. Using a large spatula, fold them in quickly, being careful not to knock out any air.

4 Fill the molds with the mixture and bake in the oven for 15 minutes or until golden brown around the edges and springy to the touch. Remove from the oven and transfer to a wire rack to cool before dusting with confectioner's sugar.

STORE The madeleines will keep in an airtight container for 1 day.

BAKER'S TIP
These delightful little treats are meant to be as light as air. Care should be taken to incorporate as much air as possible into the batter at the whisking stage, and to lose as little volume from the batter when folding in the flour. Best eaten the same day.

Scones

Homemade scones are one of the simplest and best afternoon treats. Buttermilk makes the lightest scones.

MAKES 6–8

15–20 MINS

12–15 MINS

UP TO 4 WEEKS

Special equipment
3in (7cm) pastry cutter

Ingredients
4 tbsp unsalted butter,
  chilled and cut into pieces,
  plus extra for greasing
1¾ cups all-purpose flour,
  plus extra for dusting
2 tsp baking powder
½ tsp salt
⅔ cup buttermilk

1 Preheat the oven to 425°F (220°C). Line a baking sheet with parchment and grease.

2 Sift the flour, baking powder, and salt into a large chilled bowl.

3 Put the butter in the bowl, keeping all ingredients as cold as possible.

4 Rub with your fingertips until it forms fine crumbs, working quickly, lifting to aerate it.

5 Make a well in the mixture and in a slow, steady stream, pour the buttermilk into it.

6 Quickly toss the flour mixture and buttermilk with a fork. Do not over-mix.

7 Stir the mixture until the crumbs form a dough. Add a little more buttermilk if it seems dry.

8 Turn onto a floured surface and knead for a few seconds. Keep it rough, not smooth.

9 Pat the dough out to a round ½in (1cm) thick, keeping it as cool and unworked as you can.

SMALL CAKES

122

10 Cut out rounds with the pastry cutter; see Baker's Tip, page 124.

11 Pat out the trimmings and cut additional rounds until all the dough has been used.

12 Arrange the scones so they are about 2in (5cm) apart on the prepared baking sheet.

13 Bake in the preheated oven for 12–15 minutes, until lightly browned and risen. Scones should be eaten the day they are baked, ideally still warm from the oven, and spread with butter, jam, and clotted cream.

Scone variations

Currant Scones

Serve these currant-studded scones straight from the oven, spread with butter or clotted cream.

| MAKES 6 | 15–20 MINS | 12–15 MINS | UP TO 4 WEEKS |

Ingredients
4 tbsp unsalted butter, chilled and diced, plus extra for greasing
1 large egg yolk, for glazing
⅔ cup buttermilk, plus 1 tbsp for glazing
1¾ cups all-purpose flour, plus extra for dusting
2 tsp baking powder
½ tsp salt
¼ tsp baking soda
2 tsp sugar
2 tbsp currants

Method
1 Preheat the oven to 425°F (220°C), and grease a baking sheet with butter. Beat the egg yolk and the 1 tablespoon buttermilk together and set aside.

2 Sift the flour, baking powder, salt, and baking soda into a bowl and add the sugar. Add the butter and rub the mixture with your fingertips until it forms fine crumbs. Stir in the currants. Pour in the buttermilk and quickly toss the mixture with a fork to form crumbs. Stir just until the crumbs hold together and form a dough.

3 Transfer the dough to a floured work surface. Cut it in half and pat each half into a 6in (15cm) round, about ½in (1cm) thick. With a sharp knife, cut each round into 4 wedges. Arrange the wedges about 2in (5cm) apart on the prepared baking sheet. Brush them with the glaze.

4 Bake the scones in the heated oven until lightly browned, 12–15 minutes. Leave for a few minutes on the baking sheet, then transfer to a wire rack to cool.

BAKER'S TIP
One of the secrets to well-risen scones is in the way they are cut. It is best to use a sharp pastry cutter or knife, as here, preferably made of metal. They should be cut with a strong downward motion, and the cutter should not be twisted at all when cutting. This ensures a high, even rise when cooking.

Cheese and Parsley Scones

Basic scone mix is easily adapted for a tasty savory variation.

| 20 SMALL OR 6 BIG | 20 MINS | 8–10 MINS | UP TO 12 WEEKS |

Special equipment
1½in (4cm) pastry cutter for mini scones, or 2½in (6cm) pastry cutter for large scones

Ingredients
oil, for greasing
1¾ cups all-purpose flour, sifted, plus extra for dusting
1 tsp baking powder
pinch of salt
4 tbsp unsalted butter, chilled and cubed
1 tsp dried parsley
1 tsp black peppercorns, crushed
2oz (50g) aged Cheddar cheese, grated
½ cup milk

Method
1 Preheat the oven to 425°F (220°C). Lightly oil a medium-sized baking sheet. In a large bowl, mix together the flour, baking powder, and salt. Add the butter and, using your fingertips, rub it in until the mixture resembles fine bread crumbs.

2 Stir in the parsley, peppercorns, and half the cheese, then add enough milk to bind and make the dough come together (reserve the rest for brushing on the top of the scones). Mix into a soft dough.

3 Roll out the dough on a lightly floured board to a thickness of about ¾in (2cm). Using your chosen pastry cutter, cut out rounds. Set them on the prepared baking sheet, brush with the remaining milk, and sprinkle with the remaining cheese.

4 Bake on the top rack of the oven for 8–10 minutes until golden. Leave on the baking sheet for a couple of minutes to cool a little, then either serve warm or cool completely on a wire rack.

Strawberry Shortcakes

These shortcakes are perfect served as a light summer dessert.

MAKES 6 | **15–20 MINS** | **12–15 MINS** | **4 WEEKS, UNFILLED**

Special equipment
3in (8cm) pastry cutter

Ingredients
4 tbsp unsalted butter, cut into pieces, plus extra
1¾ cups all-purpose flour, plus extra for dusting
1 tbsp baking powder
½ tsp salt
¼ cup sugar
⅔ cup heavy cream, plus extra if needed

For the coulis
1lb 2oz (500g) strawberries, hulled
2–3 tbsp confectioner's sugar
2 tbsp Kirsch (optional)

For the filling
1lb 2oz (500g) strawberries, hulled and sliced
¼ cup sugar, plus 2–3 tbsp
1 cup heavy cream
1 tsp pure vanilla extract

Method

1 Preheat the oven to 425°F (220°C). Butter a baking sheet. Sift the flour into a bowl with the baking powder and salt, and stir in the sugar. Rub to form crumbs. Add the cream, tossing; add more, if dry. Add the butter and rub in with your fingertips to form crumbs.

2 Press the crumbs together to form a ball of dough. On a floured surface, lightly knead the dough. Pat out a round, ½in (1cm) thick, and cut out 6 rounds with the cutter (see Baker's Tip). Transfer to the baking sheet and bake for 12–15 minutes. Cool on a wire rack.

3 For the coulis, purée the strawberries, then stir in the confectioner's sugar and Kirsch.

4 For the filling, mix the strawberries and sugar. Whip the cream until soft peaks form. Add 2–3 tablespoons of sugar and the vanilla. Whip until stiff. Cut the cakes in half. Put the strawberries on the bottom halves, followed by the cream. Top each with its lid. Pour the coulis around. Serve immediately.

Welsh Cakes

These traditional small cakes from Wales take minutes to prepare and cook, and you don't even have to remember to preheat the oven.

| 24 SMALL CAKES | 20 MINS | 16–24 MINS | UP TO 4 WEEKS |

Special equipment
2in (5cm) pastry cutter

Ingredients
1⅓ cups all-purpose flour, plus extra for dusting
1½ tsp baking powder
½ tsp salt
7 tbsp unsalted butter, chilled and diced
⅓ cup sugar, plus extra for dusting
½ cup golden raisins
1 large egg, at room temperature, beaten
a little milk, if needed

Method

1 Sift the flour, baking powder, and salt into a large bowl. Rub the butter into the flour until the mixture resembles fine bread crumbs. Mix in the sugar and the golden raisins. Pour in the egg.

2 Mix the ingredients together, bringing the mixture into a ball using your hands. This should be firm enough to roll out, but if it seems too stiff you can add a little milk.

3 On a floured work surface, gently roll out the dough to about ¼in (5mm) thick, and cut disks out of the dough, using the pastry cutter. Heat a large, heavy-bottomed frying pan, cast iron skillet, or flat grill pan over medium-low heat.

4 Cook the cakes, in batches, in a little melted butter for 2–3 minutes each side, until they puff up, are golden brown, and are cooked through. While still warm, dust the cakes with a little sugar before serving. (Note that Welsh cakes are best eaten immediately. If you freeze them, be sure to reheat in the oven after defrosting.)

BAKER'S TIP
These are a delightfully easy afternoon treat, and can be ready to eat within minutes of starting. The secret is to cook them over a fairly low heat, and to be extremely careful when turning them over to cook on the second side. Delicious eaten immediately with butter.

Rock Cakes

It's high time these classic British buns enjoyed a renaissance. Correctly cooked, they are light, crumbly, and incredibly simple to make.

| MAKES 12 | 15 MINS | 15–20 MINS | UP TO 4 WEEKS |

Ingredients
1½ cups all-purpose flour
1½ tsp baking powder

½ tsp salt
7 tbsp unsalted butter, chilled and diced
⅓ cup sugar
¾ cup (4oz) mixed dried fruit (raisins, golden raisins, and mixed peel)
2 large eggs
2 tbsp milk, plus extra if needed
½ tsp pure vanilla extract

Method

1 Preheat the oven to 375°F (190°C). In a large bowl, rub together the flour, baking powder, salt, and butter until the mixture resembles fine bread crumbs. Mix in the sugar. Add the dried fruit to the bowl and mix together throughly.

2 In a bowl, whisk together the eggs, milk, and vanilla extract. Make a well in the center of the flour mixture and pour the egg mixture into the middle. Mix thoroughly to combine, producing a firm mixture. Use a little more milk if the mixture seems too stiff.

3 Line 2 baking sheets with parchment paper. Place large tablespoons of the mixture on to the baking sheets, leaving plenty of space for the cakes to spread. Bake the cakes in the center of the oven for 15–20 minutes until they are golden brown. Remove to a wire rack to cool slightly.

4 Serve warm, split, and spread with butter or jam. Rock cakes should be eaten the day they are baked as they do not store well.

BAKER'S TIP

Easy-to-make rock cakes are named after their classic, rugged shape, rather than their texture! Make sure that the mixture is piled at least 2–3in (5–7cm) high on the baking sheet, which will ensure the classic rough edges even after they have spread out on baking.

Profiteroles

These cream-filled choux pastry buns, drizzled with chocolate sauce, make a deliciously decadent dessert.

SERVES 4 | **30 MINS** | **22 MINS** | **12 WEEKS, UNFILLED**

Special equipment
2 piping bags with a ½in (1cm) plain nozzle and ¼in (5mm) star nozzle

Ingredients

For the choux buns
½ cup all-purpose flour
4 tbsp unsalted butter
2 large eggs, beaten

For the filling and topping
1¾ cup heavy cream
7oz (200g) good-quality dark chocolate, broken into pieces
2 tbsp butter
2 tbsp corn syrup

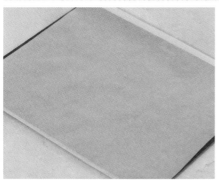

1 Preheat the oven to 425°F (220°C). Line 2 large baking sheets with parchment paper.

2 Sift the flour into a large bowl, holding the sieve up high to aerate the flour.

3 Put the butter and ⅔ cup water into a small saucepan and heat gently until melted.

4 Bring to a boil, remove from the heat, and add in the flour all at once.

5 Beat with a wooden spoon until smooth; the mixture should form a ball. Cool for 10 minutes.

6 Gradually add the eggs, beating very well after each addition to incorporate.

7 Continue adding the egg, little by little, to form a stiff, smooth, and shiny paste.

8 Spoon the mixture into a piping bag fitted with a ½in (1cm) plain nozzle.

9 Pipe walnut-sized rounds, set well apart. Bake for 20 minutes until risen and golden.

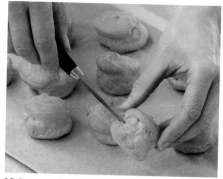

10 Remove from the oven and slit the side of each bun to allow the steam to escape.

11 Return to the oven for 2 minutes to crisp, then transfer to a wire rack to cool completely.

12 Before serving, pour ½ cup cream into a saucepan and whip the rest until just peaking.

13 Add the chocolate, butter, and syrup to the cream in the pan and heat gently until melted.

14 Pile the whipped cream into a piping bag fitted with a ¼in (5mm) star nozzle.

15 Pipe cream into each choux bun and arrange onto a serving plate or cake stand.

16 Stir the sauce well, pour it over the buns, and serve immediately.
PREPARE AHEAD The unfilled buns will keep in an airtight container for 2 days.

Choux Pastry variations

Chocolate Orange Profiteroles

A delicious twist on the original, heightened by sharp orange zest and liqueur. Try to use dark chocolate that is at least 60 percent cocoa solids for a bitter chocolate orange taste.

SERVES 6	20 MINS	30–35 MINS	12 WEEKS, UNFILLED

Special equipment
2 piping bags with a ½in (1cm) plain nozzle and ¼in (5mm) star nozzle

Ingredients

For the choux buns
4 tbsp unsalted butter, plus extra for greasing
¾ cup all-purpose flour, sifted
2 large eggs, beaten

For the chocolate sauce
6oz (150g) good-quality dark chocolate, broken into pieces
1¼ cups half-and-half
2 tbsp corn syrup
1 tbsp Grand Marnier

For the filling
2 cups heavy whipping cream
finely grated zest of 1 large orange
2 tbsp Grand Marnier

Method

1 Preheat the oven to 425°F (220°C). Grease 2 baking sheets. To make the choux pastry, melt the butter with 1¼ cups water in a pan, then bring to a boil. As soon as the mixture comes to a boil, remove from the heat and add the flour. Beat hard with a wooden spoon until the mixture is thick and glossy and comes away from the sides of the pan. Gradually beat in the egg a little at a time until the mixture is smooth, thick, and shiny; it should drop easily off the spoon.

2 Fit the piping bag with the plain nozzle and pipe walnut-sized rounds, well spaced apart on the baking sheets. Bake for 10–15 minutes, or until puffed up, then reduce the heat to 375°F (190°C) and bake for another 20 minutes, or until crisp and golden. Remove from the oven and make slits in the sides for the air to escape. Return to the oven for a few minutes so that the centers dry out. Cool completely on a wire rack.

3 To make the filling, whisk the cream, orange zest, and Grand Marnier in a bowl until just thicker than soft peaks. Fill the profiteroles with the cream using the piping bag with star nozzle.

4 To make the chocolate sauce, melt the chocolate, cream, syrup, and Grand Marnier together in a small pan, whisking until the sauce is smooth and glossy. Serve the profiteroles with the hot sauce spooned over.

PREPARE AHEAD The unfilled buns will keep in an airtight container for 2 days.

BAKER'S TIP
Immediately after removing choux pastries from the oven, it is vital to create a slit in each to allow the steam to escape. This will result in an open-textured, dry, and crisp pastry. If you do not slit the pastries, the steam will remain inside and the buns will be soggy.

Cheese Gougères with Smoked Salmon

These savory choux pastry puffs are a traditional dish of the Burgundy region of France, where they are displayed in almost every bakery window. Stuffed with smoked salmon, they make sophisticated canapés.

SERVES 8	40–45 MINS	30–35 MINS

Ingredients
5 tbsp unsalted butter, diced, extra for greasing
1¼ tsp salt
1 cup all-purpose flour, sifted
5–6 large eggs
5oz (125g) Gruyère cheese, coarsely grated

For the smoked salmon filling
salt and pepper
2¼lb (1kg) fresh spinach, trimmed and washed
2 tbsp unsalted butter
1 onion, finely chopped
4 garlic cloves, finely chopped
pinch of ground nutmeg
1 cup cream cheese
6oz (175g) smoked salmon, sliced into strips
4 tbsp milk

Method

1 Preheat the oven to 375°F (190°C). Grease 2 baking sheets. Melt the butter in a pan with 1 cup water and ¾ teaspoon of salt. Bring to a boil. Remove from the heat and add the flour. Beat until the mixture is smooth. Return the pan to the stove and beat over low heat for 30 seconds to dry out the dough.

2 Remove from the heat. Add 4 eggs, 1 at a time, beating after each. Beat the fifth egg in a separate bowl and add gradually until the dough is shiny and soft. Stir in half the cheese. Place 8 x 2½in (6cm) mounds of dough on the baking sheets, leaving room for the dough to spread as it bakes. Beat the remaining egg and salt. Brush over each of the puffs.

3 Bring a saucepan of salted water to a boil. Add the spinach and wilt for 1–2 minutes. Drain. When cool, squeeze to remove any water, then finely chop. Melt the butter in a frying pan. Add the onion and cook until soft. Add the garlic, nutmeg, salt, and pepper to taste, and the spinach. Keep cooking, stirring, until any liquid has evaporated. Add the cream cheese and stir until the mixture is thoroughly combined. Remove from the heat.

4 Add two-thirds of the smoked salmon, pour in the milk, and stir. Mound 2–3 tablespoons of filling into each cheese puff. Put the rest of the salmon on top. Rest the lid against the side of each puff and serve.

Chocolate Éclairs

These cousins of the profiterole can be easily adapted: try the chocolate orange topping and orange cream filling (see opposite), or filling with crème pâtissière or chocolate crème pâtissière.

MAKES 30   **30 MINS**   **25–30 MINS**   **12 WEEKS, UNFILLED**

Special equipment
piping bag with ½in (1cm) plain nozzle

Ingredients
5 tbsp unsalted butter
1 cup all-purpose flour, sifted
3 large eggs
2 cups heavy whipping cream
6oz (150g) good-quality dark chocolate

Method
1 Preheat the oven to 400°F (200°C). Melt the butter in a pan with ¾ cup cold water, then bring to a boil, remove from the heat, and stir in the flour. Beat with a wooden spoon until well combined.

2 Lightly beat the eggs and add to the flour and butter mixture a little at a time, whisking constantly. Continue whisking until the mixture is smooth and glossy and comes away easily from the sides of the pan. Transfer to the piping bag.

3 Pipe 4in (10cm) lengths of the mixture on to 2 baking sheets lined with parchment paper, cutting the end of the length of pastry from the bag with a wet knife. You should have around 30 in all. Bake for 20–25 minutes or until golden brown, then remove from the oven and make a slit down the side of each. Return to the oven for 5 minutes for the insides to cook through. Then remove and leave to cool.

4 Put the cream in a mixing bowl and whisk until soft peaks form. Spoon or pipe into each éclair. Break the chocolate into pieces and place in a heatproof bowl. Sit the bowl over a pan of simmering water (making sure the bowl does not touch the water) and stir until the chocolate is melted and smooth. Spoon over the éclairs and serve.

PREPARE AHEAD The unfilled éclairs will keep in an airtight container for 2 days.

Raspberry Cream Swiss Meringues

These mini meringues are filled with fresh raspberries and whipped cream, perfect for a summer buffet.

MAKES
6–8

10 MINS

1 HOUR

Special equipment
metal mixing bowl (optional)
piping bag with plain nozzle
  (optional)

Ingredients
4 egg whites (each medium egg
  white will weigh about 1oz/30g)
about 1 cup sugar, see step 3

For the filling
4oz (100g) raspberries
1 cup heavy cream
1 tbsp confectioner's sugar, sifted

SMALL CAKES

1 Preheat the oven to around 250°F (120°C). Line a baking sheet with parchment paper.

2 Make sure the metal bowl is clean and dry. Use a lemon to remove traces of grease.

3 Weigh the egg whites. You will need exactly double the weight of sugar to egg whites.

4 Whisk the egg whites in the metal bowl until they are stiff and form strong peaks.

5 Gradually add half the sugar, a couple of tablespoons at a time, whisking in between.

6 Gently fold the remaining sugar into the egg whites, trying to lose as little air as possible.

7 Put tablespoons of the mixture onto the baking sheet leaving 2in (5cm) gaps between.

8 Alternatively, pipe with a plain nozzle. Bake in the center of the oven for 1 hour.

9 They are ready when they lift easily from the parchment and sound hollow when tapped.

10 Turn off the oven and leave the meringues to cool inside. Remove to a wire rack until cold.

11 Put the raspberries in a bowl and crush them with the back of a fork, so they break up.

12 In a separate bowl whisk up the cream until firm but not stiff.

13 Gently fold together the cream and crushed raspberries. Mix with the confectioner's sugar.

14 Spread a little of the raspberry mixture onto half the meringues.

15 Top with the remaining meringue halves and gently press together to form sandwiches.

For sweet canapés, pipe smaller meringues and reduce the cooking time to 45 minutes; makes about 20 sandwiches. **PREPARE AHEAD** Keep unfilled in an airtight container for 5 days.

Meringue variations

Giant Pistachio Meringues

Too large to sandwich with cream, these beautiful creations are eaten like oversized cookies.

MAKES 8   **15 MINS**   **1½ HOURS**

Special equipment
food processor with blade attachment
large metal mixing bowl

Ingredients
4 egg whites, at room temperature
about 1 cup sugar, see page 134, step 3
4oz (100g) unsalted, shelled pistachios

Method

1 Preheat the oven to the lowest setting, around 250°F (120°C). Spread the pistachios on a baking sheet and bake for 5 minutes then transfer them to a kitchen towel and rub to remove excess skin. Cool. Finely grind just less than half the nuts in a food processor, and coarsely chop the rest.

2 Put the egg whites into the metal bowl and whisk with an electric hand mixer until stiff peaks form. Add the sugar 2 tablespoons at a time, whisking between additions, until you have added at least half. Fold in the remaining sugar and the ground pistachios. Try to lose as little air as possible.

3 Line a baking sheet with parchment paper. Put large heaping tablespoons of the meringue mixture on to the sheet, leaving at least 2in (5cm) gaps between them. Scatter the tops with the chopped pistachios.

4 Bake in the center of the oven for 1½ hours. Turn off the oven and leave the meringues to cool inside, to prevent them from cracking. Transfer the meringues from the oven to a wire rack to cool completely.

5 Serve the meringues piled on top of each other, for maximum impact.

STORE These will keep in an airtight container for 3 days.

Lemon and Praline Meringues

Similar to Monts Blancs (see right), these have added crunch.

SERVES 6   **35 MINS**   **1½ HOURS**

Special equipment
piping bag with star nozzle

Ingredients
3 egg whites, at room temperature
pinch of salt
about ¾ cup sugar, see page 134, step 3, plus an extra ¼ cup
vegetable oil, for greasing
2oz (60g) whole blanched almonds
pinch of cream of tartar
3oz (85g) dark chocolate, chopped
⅔ cup heavy cream
3 tbsp lemon curd

Method

1 Preheat the oven to 250°F (120°C) and line a baking sheet with parchment paper. Whisk the egg whites with the salt until stiff. Add 2 tablespoons sugar, and whisk until smooth and shiny. Add sugar, 1 tablespoon at a time, whisking well after each addition. Spoon into the piping bag, and pipe 6 x 4in (10cm) circles onto the baking sheet. Bake for 1½ hours, or until crisp.

2 Meanwhile, make the praline. Grease a baking sheet and put the ¼ cup sugar, almonds, and cream of tartar into a small, heavy saucepan. Set the pan over low heat and stir until the sugar dissolves. Boil until the syrup turns golden, then pour out onto the greased baking sheet. Leave until completely cold, then coarsely chop.

3 Melt the chocolate in a bowl set over simmering water. Whip the cream until just holding a trail, and fold in the lemon curd. Spread each meringue with chocolate. Allow to set, then pile the lemon curd cream on top, sprinkle with praline, and serve.

PREPARE AHEAD The meringue bases will keep in an airtight container for 5 days.

SMALL CAKES

Monts Blancs

If using sweetened chestnut purée, omit the sugar in the filling.

MAKES 8 | **20 MINS** | **45–60 MINS**

Special equipment
large metal mixing bowl
4in (10cm) pastry cutter

Ingredients
4 egg whites, at room temperature
about 1 cup sugar, see page 134, step 3
sunflower oil, for greasing

For the filling
14oz (435g) can unsweetened chestnut puree,
  or sweetened
½ cup sugar
1 tsp pure vanilla extract
2 cups heavy cream
confectioner's sugar, to dust

Method

1 Preheat the oven to the lowest setting, around 250°F (120°C).

2 Put the egg whites into a large, clean metal bowl and whisk them until they are stiff and leave peaks when the whisk is removed from the egg whites. Gradually add the sugar 2 tablespoons at a time, whisking well between each addition, until you have added at least half. Gently fold the remaining sugar into the egg whites, trying to lose as little air as possible.

3 Lightly grease the pastry cutter. Line 2 baking sheets with parchment paper. Place the pastry cutter on the sheets, and spoon the meringue mixture into the ring, to a depth of 1¼in (3cm). Smooth over the top and gently remove the ring. Repeat until there are 4 meringue bases on each baking sheet.

4 Bake the meringues in the center of the oven for 45 minutes if you like them chewy, otherwise bake for 1 hour. Turn off the oven and leave the meringues to cool inside, to prevent them from cracking. Transfer to a wire rack to cool completely.

5 Put the chestnut purée in a bowl with the sugar (if using), vanilla, and 4 tablespoons of heavy cream, and beat together until smooth. Push through a fine sieve to make a really light, fluffy filling. In a separate bowl whisk the remaining heavy cream until firm.

6 Gently smooth 1 tablespoon chestnut filling over the top of the meringues, using a palette knife to smooth the surface. Top each meringue with a spoonful of whipped cream, smoothed with a palette knife to give the appearance of soft peaks. Dust with confectioner's sugar and serve.

PREPARE AHEAD The meringue bases can be prepared 5 days ahead and stored in an airtight container.

BAKER'S TIP
Make sure that the bowl you are using to whisk the egg whites in is completely clean and dry. For absolute accuracy, it is best to weigh the egg whites. You will need precisely double the weight of sugar to egg whites. An electronic scale is best.

cookies
& slices

Hazelnut and Raisin Oat Cookies

These cookies are an ideal cookie jar staple—tasty enough to please the kids and healthy enough for the adults.

MAKES 18 | 20 MINS | 10–15 MINS | UP TO 8 WEEKS

Ingredients

¾ cup (4oz/115g) hazelnuts
7 tbsp unsalted butter, softened
1¼ cup light brown sugar
1 large egg (room temperature), beaten
1 tsp pure vanilla extract

1 tbsp honey
¾ cup all-purpose flour, sifted
½ tsp baking powder
1½ cups oats
¼ tsp salt
⅔ cup raisins
a little milk, if needed

1 Preheat the oven to 375°F (190°C). Toast the hazelnuts on a baking sheet for 5 minutes.

2 Once toasted, rub with a clean tea towel to remove most of the skins.

3 Roughly chop the hazelnuts and then set aside.

4 In a bowl, cream together the butter and sugar with an electric hand mixer until smooth.

5 Add the egg, vanilla extract, and honey, and beat well until smooth once more.

6 Combine the flour, baking soda, oats, and salt in a separate large bowl, and stir to mix.

7 Stir the flour mixture into the creamed mixture and beat until very well combined.

8 Add the chopped nuts and raisins, and mix until evenly distributed throughout the dough.

9 If the mixture is too stiff to work with easily, add a little milk until it becomes pliable.

10 Line 2 or 3 baking sheets with parchment paper. Roll the dough into walnut-sized balls.

11 Flatten each ball slightly, leaving plenty of space between them.

12 Bake in batches for 10–15 minutes until golden. Cool slightly, then move to a wire rack.

13 Leave to cool completely before serving. **STORE** The cookies will keep in an airtight container for 5 days, so if you make a batch on Sunday night they will last the school and working week.

Cookie variations

Pistachio and Cranberry Oat Cookies

The jewel colors of the pistachios and cranberries gleam out from these slightly more grown up versions of the classic fruit and nut cookies.

| MAKES 24 | 20 MINS | 10–15 MINS | UP TO 8 WEEKS |

Ingredients

1 cup (4oz) pistachio nuts
7 tbsp unsalted butter, softened
1¼ cups light brown sugar
1 large egg
1 tsp pure vanilla extract
1 tbsp honey
¾ cup all-purpose flour, sifted
½ tsp baking soda
1½ cups oats
¼ tsp of salt
¾ cup (4oz) dried cranberries, chopped
2–3 tbsp milk, if needed

Method

1 Preheat the oven to 375°F (190°C). Place the pistachios on a baking sheet and toast them in the oven for 5 minutes, then remove and coarsely chop.

2 Combine the butter and sugar in a bowl and cream with an electric hand mixer until smooth. Add the egg, vanilla extract, and honey and beat well until smooth.

3 Stir in the flour, baking soda, oats, and salt to combine. Add the chopped nuts and cranberries, mixing them into the cookie dough with your hands, if necessary. If the mixture is too stiff, add a little milk.

4 Take walnut-sized pieces and roll them into a ball between your palms. Flatten them slightly and place on 2 or 3 non-stick baking sheets, leaving space for the cookies to spread. Bake for 10–15 minutes until golden brown (you may need to do this in batches). Leave on the sheets for a couple of minutes before transferring to a wire rack to cool completely.

STORE The cookies will keep in an airtight container for 5 days.

BAKER'S TIP

Once you have mastered the recipe for oatmeal cookies, try experimenting with different combinations of fresh or dried fruit and nuts, or adding seeds such as sunflower seeds and pumpkin seeds into the mix.

Apple and Cinnamon Oat Cookies

Adding grated apple to the dough makes these cookies soft and chewy.

| MAKES 24 | 20 MINS | 10–15 MINS | UP TO 8 WEEKS |

Ingredients

7 tbsp unsalted butter, softened
1¼ cups light brown sugar
1 large egg
1 tsp pure vanilla extract
1 tbsp honey
¾ cup all-purposed flour, sifted
½ tsp baking powder
1½ cups oats
2 tsp cinnamon
¼ tsp of salt
2 apples, peeled, cored, and coarsely grated
a little milk, if needed

Method

1 Preheat the oven to 375°F (190°C). Combine the butter and sugar in a bowl and cream together with an electric hand mixer until smooth. Add the egg, vanilla extract, and honey, and beat well until smooth.

2 Stir the flour, baking soda, oats, cinnamon, and salt into the creamed mixture to combine. Mix in the apple. If the mixture seems a bit too stiff, add a little milk. Take walnut-sized pieces of dough and roll them into a ball between your palms.

3 Flatten them slightly and place on 2 or 3 non-stick baking sheets, leaving space for the cookies to spread. Bake for 10–15 minutes until golden brown. Leave on the sheets for a couple of minutes before transferring them to a wire rack to cool completely.

STORE The cookies will keep in an airtight container for 5 days.

White Chocolate and Macadamia Nut Cookies

Here classic chocolate cookies are given a sophisticated twist.

| MAKES 24 | 25 MINS | 10–15 MINS | UP TO 4 WEEKS |

Chilling time
30 mins

Ingredients

6oz (150g) dark chocolate, broken into pieces
¾ cup all-purpose flour
¼ cup cocoa powder
½ tsp baking powder
¼ tsp salt
5 tbsp unsalted butter, softened
1 cup light brown sugar
1 large egg, beaten
1 tsp pure vanilla extract
⅓ cup (2oz) macadamia nuts, chopped
1¾oz (50g) white chocolate chunks

Method

1 Preheat the oven to 350°F (180°C). Melt the dark chocolate in a heatproof bowl set over a pan of simmering water. The bowl should not touch the water. Set aside to cool. Sift the flour, cocoa powder, baking powder, and salt together.

2 In a large bowl, cream together the butter and sugar with an electric hand mixer until light and fluffy. Beat in the egg and vanilla extract. Mix in the flour mixture. Add the chocolate and mix thoroughly. Finally, stir in the nuts and white chocolate chunks, wrap in plastic wrap, and chill for 30 minutes.

3 Place tablespoons of the chilled cookie dough on non-stick baking sheets, at least 2in (5cm) apart, as they will spread.

4 Bake in the top third of the oven for 10–15 minutes until cooked through but still soft in the middle. Leave on the sheets for a few minutes, then transfer to a wire rack to cool.

STORE The cookies will keep in an airtight container for 3 days.

Butter Cookies

These thin, elegant cookies are one of my favorite recipes. They are quick, simple, and decidedly addictive.

MAKES 30 | **15 MINS** | **10–15 MINS** | **UP TO 8 WEEKS**

Special equipment
2¾in (7cm) round cookie cutter
food processor with blade
attachment (optional)

Ingredients
11 tbsp unsalted butter, softened
   and diced
½ cup sugar
1½ cups all-purpose flour, sifted,
   plus extra for dusting
1 large egg yolk
1 tsp pure vanilla extract

1 Preheat the oven to 350°F (180°C). Have 2 or 3 non-stick baking sheets on hand.

2 Put the butter, sugar, and flour in a large bowl, or into the bowl of a food processor.

3 Rub together, or pulse-blend the ingredients until they look like fine bread crumbs.

4 Add the egg yolk and vanilla extract, and bring the mixture together into a dough.

5 Turn the dough out onto a lightly floured work surface and knead it briefly until smooth.

6 Flour the dough and work surface well, and roll it out to a thickness of about ¼in (5mm).

7 Use a palette knife to move the sheet of dough around, to prevent sticking.

8 If the dough is too sticky to roll well, chill for 15 minutes, then try again.

9 With the pastry cutter, cut out round cookies and transfer them to the baking sheets.

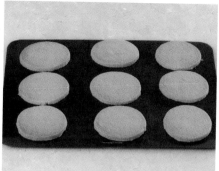

10 Re-roll the scraps to ¼in (5mm) thick, and cut out cookies until all the dough is used.

11 Bake in the preheated oven for 12–15 minutes, until golden brown at the edges.

12 Leave the cookies to cool until firm enough to handle, then transfer to a wire rack.

13 Leave the butter cookies to cool completely on the wire rack, before serving. **STORE** The cookies will keep well in an airtight container for 5 days.

Butter Cookie variations

Crystallized Ginger Cookies

Here crystallized ginger adds warmth and depth of flavor.

MAKES 30 | 15 MINS | 12–15 MINS | UP TO 8 WEEKS

Special equipment
food processor with blade attachment (optional)
3in (7cm) round cookie cutter

Ingredients
11 tbsp unsalted butter, softened and diced
½ cup sugar
1½ cups all-purpose flour, sifted, extra for dusting
1 tsp ground ginger
2oz (50g) crystallized ginger, finely chopped
1 large egg yolk
1 tsp pure vanilla extract

Method

1 Preheat the oven to 350°F (180°C). Combine the butter, sugar, and flour in a bowl, or in the bowl of a food processor fitted with a blade, and rub or process together until the mixture forms fine crumbs. Stir in the ground and crystallized gingers.

2 Add the egg yolk and vanilla extract, and bring the mixture together into a dough. Turn out onto a lightly floured work surface and knead it together briefly to form a smooth dough. Flour the dough and work surface lightly, and roll it out to ¼in (5mm) thick. Cut out cookies with the cookie cutter and transfer them to several non-stick baking sheets.

3 Bake in the oven for 12–15 minutes until they are golden brown at the edges. Leave on the baking sheets for a few minutes, then transfer to a wire rack to cool completely.

STORE The cookies will keep in an airtight container for 5 days.

Almond Butter Cookies

The addition of almond extract makes these delicious cookies quite grown up and not overly sweet.

MAKES 30 | 15 MINS | 12–15 MINS | UP TO 8 WEEKS

Special equipment
3in (7cm) round cookie cutter
food processor with blade attachment (optional)

Ingredients
11 tbsp unsalted butter, softened and diced
½ cup sugar
1½ cups all-purpose flour, sifted, extra for dusting
⅓ cup sliced almonds, lightly toasted if preferred
1 tsp almond extract
1 large egg yolk

Method

1 Preheat the oven to 350°F (180°C). Combine the butter, sugar, and flour in a bowl, or in the bowl of a food processor with a blade attachment. Rub or process together until it forms fine crumbs. Mix in the almonds.

2 Add the egg yolk and almond extract, and bring the mixture together into a dough. Knead briefly to form a smooth dough. Roll out to ¼in (5mm) thick.

3 Cut out cookies with the cookie cutter and transfer to several non-stick baking sheets. Bake in the oven for 12–15 minutes until golden brown at the edges. Leave for a few minutes, then transfer to a wire rack to cool.

STORE The cookies will keep in an airtight container for 5 days.

> **BAKER'S TIP**
> Always look for almond extract, as bottles labeled "essence" are made from synthetic flavorings. For excellent after-dinner cookies to have with coffee, roll the cookies out as thin as you dare and bake for 5–8 minutes only.

Spritzgebäck Cookies

These delicate, buttery cookies are based on a traditional German cookie popular at Christmas. ▶

MAKES 45 | 45 MINS | 15 MINS

Special equipment
cookie press, or piping bag and star nozzle

Ingredients
28 tbsp unsalted butter, softened
1 cup sugar
few drops of pure vanilla extract
pinch of salt
3¼ cups all-purpose flour, sifted
1¼ cups ground almonds
4oz (100g) dark or milk chocolate

Method

1 Preheat the oven to 350°F (180°C). Line 2–3 large baking sheets with parchment paper. Place the butter in a bowl and beat until smooth. Stir in the sugar, vanilla extract, and salt until the mixture is thick and the sugar is absorbed. Add two-thirds of the flour, stirring in a little at a time.

2 Add the rest of the flour and ground almonds and knead the mixture to make a smooth dough. Shape the dough into rolls and use the cookie press or piping bag to squeeze 3in (7.5cm) lengths of the dough onto the prepared baking sheets.

3 Bake for 12 minutes, or until lightly golden, and transfer to a wire rack to cool. Melt the chocolate gently in a microwave or in a bowl over a pan of simmering water. Dip one end of the cooled cookies into the chocolate, and return to the rack to set.

STORE The cookies will keep in an airtight container for 2–3 days.

Gingerbread Men

All children love to make gingerbread men. This recipe is quick and the dough is easy for little bakers to handle.

MAKES 16 | **20 MINS** | **10–12 MINS** | **8 WEEKS, UNBAKED**

Special equipment
4½in (11cm) gingerbread man cutter
piping bag with thin nozzle (optional)

Ingredients
4 tbsp corn syrup
2⅓ cups all-purpose flour,
   plus extra for dusting
1 tsp baking soda
1½ tsp ground ginger
1½ tsp pumpkin pie spice
7 tbsp unsalted butter, softened
   and diced
¾ cup dark brown sugar
1 large egg
raisins, to decorate
confectioner's sugar, sifted (optional)

1 Preheat the oven to 375°F (190°C). Heat the corn syrup until it liquefies, then cool.

2 Sift the flour, baking soda, and spices into a large bowl. Add the butter.

3 Rub together with your fingertips until the mixture looks like fine bread crumbs.

4 Add the sugar to the bread crumbs mixture and mix well.

5 Beat the egg into the cooled syrup until well blended.

6 Make a well in the flour mixture. Pour in the syrup mix. Bring together to a rough dough.

7 On a lightly floured work surface, knead the dough briefly until smooth.

8 Flour the dough and the work surface well, then roll the dough out to ¼in (5mm) thick.

9 Using the cutter, cut out as many shapes as possible. Transfer to non-stick baking sheets.

COOKIES AND SLICES

10 Mix the scraps of dough, re-roll, and cut out more shapes, until all the dough is used.

11 Decorate the men with raisins, giving them eyes, a nose, and buttons down the front.

12 Bake for 10–12 minutes until golden. Transfer to a wire rack to cool completely.

13 If using, mix some confectioner's sugar in a bowl with enough water to form a thin icing.

14 Transfer the icing into the piping bag; placing the bag into a glass first will help.

15 Decorate the men with the piped icing to resemble clothes, hair, or whatever you prefer.

16 Leave the icing to set completely before serving or storing. **STORE** These gingerbread men will keep in an airtight container for 3 days.

Gingerbread variations

Swedish Spice Cookies

A version of the traditional Swedish Christmas cookies. Roll them as thin as you dare (and bake for less time) for a truly authentic result.

MAKES 60	20 MINS	10 MINS	8 WEEKS, UNBAKED

Chilling time
1 hr

Special equipment
3in (7cm) heart or star cookie cutters

Ingredients
9 tbsp unsalted butter, softened
⅔ cup sugar
1 large egg
1 tbsp corn syrup
1 tbsp light molasses
1⅓ cups all-purpose flour, plus extra for dusting
pinch of salt
1 tsp ground cinnamon
1 tsp ground ginger
1 tsp pumpkin pie spice

Method

1 With an electric hand mixer, cream the butter and sugar. Beat in the egg, corn syrup, and molasses. Sift together the flour, salt, and spices in a separate bowl. Add the flour mixture to the cookie batter and bring it all together to form a rough dough.

2 Briefly knead until smooth, place in a plastic bag, and chill for 1 hour.

3 Preheat the oven to 350°F (180°C). Roll the cookie dough out on a lightly floured surface to a thickness of ⅛in (3mm) and cut out heart or star shapes with the cookie cutters.

4 Transfer the cookies to several non-stick baking sheets and bake in the top third of the oven for 10 minutes until edges darken slightly. Leave the sheets for a few minutes, then transfer to a wire rack to cool.

STORE The cookies will keep in an airtight container for 5 days.

BAKER'S TIP
These are based on a Swedish Christmas cookie called *Pepparkakor*. To decorate a Christmas tree in traditional Swedish style, cut the cookies into heart shapes and use a straw to cut a hole out of the top before cooking. Once baked, you can tie the cookies on to the tree using red ribbon.

Gingernut Cookies

The addition of chopped nuts makes these cookies extra special.

MAKES 45	30 MINS	8–10 MINS	8 WEEKS, UNBAKED

Special equipment
3in (7cm) cookie cutters (any shape)

Ingredients
1⅓ cups all-purpose flour, plus extra for dusting
2 tsp baking powder
¾ cup sugar
a few drops of pure vanilla extract
½ tsp pumpkin pie spice
2 tsp ground ginger
⅓ cup honey
1 large egg, separated
4 tsp milk
9 tbsp butter, softened and diced
1¼ cups ground almonds
chopped hazelnuts or almonds, to decorate

Method

1 Preheat the oven to 350°F (180°C). Line 2 baking sheets with parchment paper.

2 Sift the flour and baking powder into a bowl. Add all the other ingredients except the chopped nuts. With a wooden spoon, bring the mixture together to form a soft dough. Use your hands to shape the dough into a ball.

3 Roll the dough out on a lightly floured surface to ¼in (5mm) thickness. Cut out the cookies with the shaped cutters, and place on the baking sheets, spaced apart to allow them to spread. Beat the egg white and brush over the cookies, then sprinkle with the nuts. Bake for 8–10 minutes, or until lightly golden brown.

4 Remove from the oven and allow to cool on the sheet for a few minutes, then transfer to a wire rack to cool completely.

STORE These gingernut cookies will keep in an airtight container for 3 days.

Cinnamon Stars

These classic German cookies make a great last-minute Christmas gift.

MAKES 30 | 20 MINS | 12–15 MINS | 4 WEEKS, UNBAKED

Chilling time
1 hr, or overnight (optional)

Special equipment
3in (7cm) star-shaped cookie cutter

Ingredients
2 large egg whites
1¾ cups confectioner's sugar, extra for dusting
½ tsp lemon juice
1 tsp ground cinnamon
2⅔ cups ground almonds
vegetable oil, for greasing
a little milk, if needed

Method

1 Whisk the egg whites until they are stiff. Sift in the confectioner's sugar, add the lemon juice, and continue to whisk for 5 more minutes, until thick and glossy. Take out 2 tablespoons of the mixture, cover, and set aside for topping the cookies later.

2 Gently fold the ground almonds and cinnamon into the egg white and sugar mixture. Cover and refrigerate for 1 hour or overnight. At this stage it will be a thick paste, rather than a dough.

3 Preheat oven to 325°F (160°C). Dust a work surface with sugar and turn the paste out onto it. Combine the paste with some sugar to form a soft dough. Dust a rolling pin with sugar and roll out to ¼in (5mm) thick.

4 Oil the cutter and non-stick baking sheets. Cut star shapes out of the dough. Lay the cookies on the sheets. Brush a little of the meringue mix over each cookie, mixing it with a little milk, if too thick.

5 Bake in the top third of the oven for 12–15 minutes until the topping has set. Leave to cool for at least 10 minutes on the baking sheets, then transfer to a wire rack.

STORE The cookies will keep in an airtight container for 5 days.

Canestrelli

These delightful Italian cookies are as light as air and are traditionally made with a flower-shaped cutter, a fitting shape for such a delicate cookie.

| MAKES 20–30 | 20 MINS | 15–20 MINS | UP TO 4 WEEKS |

Chilling time
30 mins

Special equipment
flower-shaped, or 2 different-sized, round cookie cutters

Ingredients
3 large egg yolks, unbroken
11 tbsp unsalted butter, softened
1¼ cup confectioner's sugar, sifted
finely grated zest of ½ lemon
¾ cup potato flour
¾ cup all-purpose flour (or potato flour if you are wheat intolerant), plus extra for dusting
2 tsp baking powder
1 tsp salt

Method

1 Gently slide the egg yolks into a pan of simmering water over low heat. Poach for 5 minutes, until completely hard, then take them out of the water and set aside to cool. When they are cool, push the egg yolks through a fine metal sieve with the back of a spoon. Scrape into a small bowl.

2 Cream together the butter and confectioners' sugar with an electric hand mixer until light and fluffy. Add the egg yolks and lemon zest, and beat well to combine.

3 Sift the flours, baking powder, and salt together and add to the cookie batter, beating well to form a smooth, soft dough. Place the dough in a plastic bag and refrigerate for 30 minutes to firm up. Preheat the oven to 325°F (160°C).

4 Roll out the chilled dough on a lightly floured work surface to ½in (1cm) thick. Cut out traditional flower-shaped cookies, or other shapes. If you have no flower-shaped cutter, you can use a larger and a smaller cutter to make ring shapes instead.

5 Place the cookies on several non-stick baking sheets and bake in the top third of the oven for 15–17 minutes, until just turning golden. The canestrelli are very delicate when warm, so leave them to cool for at least 10 minutes on their baking sheets before removing to a wire rack to cool completely.

STORE The canestrelli will keep in an airtight container for 5 days.

BAKER'S TIP

These delicate cookies originate from the Liguria region of Italy. Their light texture comes from the traditional use of potato flour in the recipe. If you cannot find potato flour, an 00 grade flour (from larger supermarkets and Italian delicatessens), or even all-purpose flour, will make a good substitute.

Macaroons

These almond meringue cookies (not to be confused with French macarons) are crisp outside and chewy inside.

MAKES 24 | 10 MINS | 12–15 MINS

Special equipment
sheets of edible wafer paper

Ingredients
2 large egg whites
1 cup sugar
1¼ cups ground almonds
2 tbsp rice flour
a few drops of almond extract
24 blanched almonds

1 Preheat the oven to 350°F (180°C). Whisk the egg whites until stiff with an electric mixer.

2 Gradually whisk in the sugar, 1 tablespoon at a time, to give a thick, glossy meringue.

3 Fold in the ground almonds, rice flour, and almond extract until well combined.

4 Divide the sheets of edible wafer paper between 2 baking sheets.

5 Place 2 teaspoons in a cup of boiling water. Dry them, then use to scoop up the mixture.

6 Place 4 teaspoons of mixture, spaced apart, on each piece of edible wafer paper.

7 Keep the mixture in rounds. Put a blanched almond in the center of each cookie.

8 Bake the macaroons in the center of the oven for 12–15 minutes, or until lightly golden.

9 Transfer to a wire rack to cool completely before peeling each cookie from the paper.

Macaroons are prone to sticking, but by using edible wafer paper, it doesn't matter if it tears off with the cookie. **STORE** Although macaroons will keep for 2–3 days in an airtight container, they tend to dry out and are always best eaten on the day they are made.

Macaroon variations

Coconut Macaroons

Coconut macaroons are simple to make and completely wheat-free. I've omitted chocolate from my version so that they remain a light treat.

MAKES 18-20	20 MINS	15–20 MINS

Chilling time
2 hrs

Special equipment
sheets of edible wafer paper (optional)

Ingredients
1 large egg white
½ cup sugar
pinch of salt
½ tsp pure vanilla extract
4oz (100g) sweetened, shredded coconut

Method

1 Preheat the oven to 325°F (160°C). In a large bowl with an electric hand mixer, whisk the egg whites until stiff. Add the sugar a little at a time, whisking between each addition, until the sugar is combined and the mixture is thick and glossy.

2 Add the salt and vanilla extract, and briefly whisk again to blend.

3 Gently fold in the coconut. Cover and refrigerate for 2 hours to firm up. This will also allow the shredded coconut to hydrate and soften.

4 Line a baking sheet with parchment or wafer paper. Place heaping teaspoons of the mixture onto the baking sheet; try to keep the mixture in a small heap.

5 Bake in the middle of the oven for 15–20 minutes, until golden brown in places. Leave the macaroons to cool on the sheets for at least 10 minutes to firm up, then transfer to a wire rack to cool completely.

STORE These macaroons will keep in an airtight container for 5 days.

Chocolate Macaroons

Add cocoa powder for a chocolate version of the basic macaroon.

MAKES 24	20 MINS	15 MINS	UP TO 4 WEEKS

Chilling time
30 mins

Special equipment
sheets of edible wafer paper (optional)

Ingredients
2 large egg whites
1 cup sugar
1 cup ground almonds
2 tbsp rice flour
¼ cup cocoa powder
24 whole blanched almonds

Method

1 Preheat the oven to 350°F (180°C). In a large bowl with an electric hand mixer, whisk the egg whites until stiff. Add the sugar a little at a time, whisking between each addition, until all the sugar is combined and the mixture is thick and glossy.

2 Fold in the almonds, rice flour, and then the cocoa powder. Cover and refrigerate for 30 minutes to firm up. Line 2 baking sheets with parchment or wafer paper.

3 Place heaping teaspoons of the mixture onto the prepared baking sheets, spacing them at least 1½in (4cm) apart as they will spread. Try to keep each portion of the mixture in a small heap. Place a blanched almond in the center of each heap.

4 Bake the macaroons at the top of the oven for 12–15 minutes, until the exterior is crisp and the edges firm to the touch. Leave the macaroons to cool on the sheets for at least 5 minutes, then transfer to a wire rack to cool completely.

STORE Best eaten on the day they are made, these will keep in an airtight container for 2–3 days.

Coffee and Hazelnut Macaroons

These gorgeous little cookies are easy to prepare, infused with flavor, and look very pretty served after dinner with coffee, especially if you make them on the smaller side.

MAKES 20   **30 MINS**   **20 MINS**   **UP TO 4 WEEKS**

Chilling time
30 mins

Special equipment
food processor with blade attachment
sheets of edible wafer paper (optional)

Ingredients
2 large egg whites
1 cup sugar
6oz (150g) whole hazelnuts, shelled, plus 20 extra
2 tbsp rice flour
1 tsp strong instant espresso powder, dissolved in 1 tsp boiling water and cooled, or equivalent cooled espresso

Method

1 Preheat the oven to 350°F (180°C). Place the hazelnuts on a baking sheet and toast for 5 minutes. Put them in a kitchen towel and rub to remove skin. Set aside to cool.

2 Whisk the egg whites until stiff. Add the sugar a little at a time, whisking, until all the sugar is combined and the mixture is thick.

3 In a food processor, pulse the hazelnuts to a powder. Fold them into the meringue mixture with the rice flour, and gently fold in 1 teaspoon of the coffee mixture. Cover and refrigerate for 30 minutes to firm up.

4 Place teaspoons of the mixture onto baking sheets lined with parchment or wafer paper, spacing them at least 1½in (4cm) apart. Keep each portion in a small heap and place a whole hazelnut in the center.

5 Bake the macaroons at the top of the oven for 12–15 minutes, until crisp and coloring slightly; check after 10 minutes if making them small. Leave on the sheets for 5 minutes and transfer to a wire rack to cool.

STORE Best eaten on the day they are made, these will keep in an airtight container for 2–3 days.

BAKER'S TIP
Old-fashioned macaroons have been rather overshadowed of late by their prettier French cousins, macarons (see pages 158–163). However, macaroons are also wheat-free, easier to make, and just as pretty, in an understated kind of way.

Strawberries and Cream Macarons

The art of macaron making can seem complex, but here I have tried to devise a recipe that will suit the home cook.

MAKES 20 **30 MINS** **18–20 MINS**

Special equipment
food processor with
  blade attachment
piping bag with small,
  plain nozzle

Ingredients
¾ cup confectioner's sugar
¾ cup ground almonds
2 large egg whites,
  at room temperature
⅓ cup sugar

For the filling
¾ cup heavy cream
5–10 very large strawberries,
  preferably the same diameter as
  the macarons

1 Preheat the oven to 300°F (150°C). Line 2 baking sheets with wax paper.

2 Trace 20 x 1¼in (3cm) circles, leaving 1¼in (3cm) between circles. Invert the paper.

3 In a food processor, pulse the almonds and confectioner's sugar to a very fine meal.

4 In a large bowl, whisk the egg whites to stiff peaks using an electric hand mixer.

5 Whisking, add the sugar a little at a time, whisking well between additions.

6 The meringue mixture should be very stiff at this point, more than for a Swiss meringue.

7 Gently fold in the almond mixture a spoonful at a time, until just incorporated.

8 Transfer the macaron mix to the piping bag, placing the bag into a bowl to help.

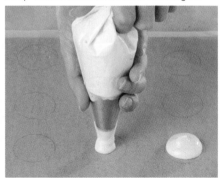

9 Using the guidelines, pipe the mix into the center of each circle, holding the bag vertically.

10 Try to keep the disks even in size and volume; the mix will spread very slightly.

11 Bang the baking sheets down a few times if there are any peaks left in the center.

12 Bake in the middle of the oven for 18–20 minutes until the surface is set firm.

13 Test one shell: a firm prod with a finger should crack the top of the macaron.

14 Leave for 15–20 minutes, then transfer to a wire rack to cool completely.

15 Whisk the cream until thickened but not stiff; it should remain succulent.

16 Transfer the cream into the (cleaned) piping bag used earlier, with the same nozzle.

17 Pipe a blob of the whipped cream onto the flat side of half the macarons.

18 Slice the strawberries across into thin slices, the same diameter as the macarons.

19 Put a slice of strawberry on top of the cream filling of each macaron.

20 Add the remaining macaron shells and sandwich gently. The fillings should peek out.

21 Serve immediately. **PREPARE AHEAD** Unfilled macaron shells can be stored for 3 days.

Macaron variations

Tangerine Macarons

Sharp, zesty tangerines are used here, rather than the more usual oranges, to counterbalance the sweetness of the meringues.

MAKES 20 | 30 MINS | 18–20 MINS

Special equipment
food processor with blade attachment

Ingredients
¾ cup confectioner's sugar
¾ cup ground almonds
1 scant tsp finely grated tangerine zest
2 large egg whites, at room temperature
⅓ cup sugar
3–4 drops orange food coloring

For the filling
¾ cup confectioner's sugar
4 tbsp unsalted butter, softened
1 tbsp tangerine juice
1 scant tsp finely grated tangerine zest

Method
1 Preheat the oven to 300°F (150°C). Line 2 baking sheets with wax paper. Draw on 1¼in (3cm) circles with a pencil, leaving a 1¼in (3cm) gap between each one. Pulse the confectioner's sugar and almonds in a food processor, until finely mixed. Add the tangerine zest and pulse briefly.

2 In a bowl, whisk the egg whites to form stiff peaks with a hand mixer. Add the sugar a little at a time, whisking well with each addition. Whisk in the food coloring.

3 Fold in the almond mixture, a spoonful at a time. Transfer to the piping bag. Holding the bag vertically, pipe meringue into the center of each circle.

4 Bake in the middle of the oven for 18–20 minutes until the surface is set firm. Leave the macarons to cool on the baking sheets for 15–20 minutes and then transfer to a wire rack to cool completely.

5 For the filling, cream together the confectioner's sugar, butter, tangerine zest, and juice until smooth. Transfer into the (cleaned) piping bag, using the same nozzle. Pipe a blob of frosting onto the flat side of half the macarons, and sandwich with the rest. Serve the same day.

PREPARE AHEAD The unfilled shells can be stored for 3 days in an airtight container.

Chocolate Macarons

These delicious macarons are filled with a rich, dark chocolate buttercream.

MAKES 20 | 30 MINS | 18–20 MINS

Special equipment
food processor with blade attachment

Ingredients
½ cup ground almonds
¼ cup cocoa powder
¾ cup confectioner's sugar
2 large egg whites, at room temperature
⅓ cup sugar

For the filling
⅓ cup cocoa powder
1¼ cups confectioner's sugar
3 tbsp unsalted butter, melted
3 tbsp milk, plus a little extra if needed

Method
1 Preheat the oven to 300°F (150°C). Line 2 baking sheets with wax paper. In a food processor, pulse together the ground almonds, cocoa powder, and confectioner's sugar until very finely mixed, with no lumps.

2 Whisk the egg whites until stiff. Add the granulated sugar, whisking. The mixture should be stiff. Fold in the almond mixture a spoonful at a time. Transfer to the piping bag. Holding the bag vertically, pipe meringue into the center of each circle.

3 Bake in the middle of the oven for 18–20 minutes. Leave to cool on the sheets 15–20 minutes, before transferring to a wire rack.

4 For the filling, sift the cocoa and confectioner's sugar into a bowl. Add the butter and milk, and whisk. Add a little milk if too thick. Transfer to the piping bag and pipe frosting onto the flat side of half the macarons and sandwich together. Serve the same day, or the macarons will go soft.

PREPARE AHEAD The unfilled shells can be stored for 3 days in an airtight container.

Raspberry Macarons

Pretty as a picture, these macarons look almost too good to eat.

MAKES 20 | 30 MINS | 18–20 MINS

Special equipment
food processor with blade attachment

Ingredients
¾ cup confectioner's sugar
¾ cup ground almonds
2 large egg whites, at room temperature
⅓ cup sugar
3–4 drops of pink food coloring

For the filling
6oz (150g) mascarpone
2 tbsp good-quality seedless raspberry conserve

Method

1 Preheat the oven to 300°F (150°C). Line 2 baking sheets with wax paper. Draw 1¼in (3cm) circles with a pencil, leaving a 1¼in (3cm) gap between each. In a food processor, pulse the confectioner's sugar and almonds until finely mixed and smooth.

2 In a bowl, whisk the egg whites until they form stiff peaks. Add the sugar, a little at a time, whisking well between each addition. Whisk in the food coloring.

3 Fold in the almond mixture a spoonful at a time, until just mixed. Transfer the mix to the piping bag. Holding the bag vertically, pipe meringue into the center of each circle.

4 Bake in the middle of the oven for 18–20 minutes until the surface is firm. Leave to cool on the sheets for 15–20 minutes, before transferring to a wire rack to cool.

5 For the filling, beat the mascarpone and raspberry conserve until smooth and transfer to the (cleaned) piping bag used earlier, with the same nozzle. Pipe a blob of the filling onto the flat side of half the macarons and sandwich together with the rest of the halves. Serve the same day, or the macarons will go soft.

PREPARE AHEAD The unfilled shells can be stored for 3 days in an airtight container.

BAKER'S TIP
The skill in making macarons comes in the technique, not in the proportions of the ingredients. Gentle folding, a heavy, flat baking sheet, and piping completely vertically downward should all help you to produce the perfect macaron.

Vanillekipferl

These crescent-shaped German cookies are often served at the same time as Cinnamon Stars (see page 151), making a truly festive platter.

| MAKES 30 | 35 MINS | 15–17 MINS | UP TO 4 WEEKS |

Chilling time
30 mins

Ingredients
1½ cup flour, plus extra for dusting
11 tbsp unsalted butter, softened and diced
⅔ cup confectioner's sugar
¾ cup ground almonds
1 tsp pure vanilla extract
1 large egg, beaten

Method

1 Sift the flour into a large bowl. Rub in the softened butter until the mixture resembles fine crumbs. Sift in the confectioner's sugar and add the ground almonds.

2 Add the vanilla extract to the egg, then pour it into the flour mixture. Bring the mixture together to form a soft dough, adding a little more flour if the mixture is very sticky. Place the dough into a plastic bag and chill it for at least 30 minutes, to firm up.

3 Preheat the oven to 325°F (160°C). Divide the dough into 2 parts, and on a lightly floured work surface, roll each part into a sausage shape, approximately 1½in (3cm) in diameter. Use a sharp knife to cut ½in (1cm) pieces from the dough.

4 To form the cookies, take a piece of the dough and roll it between your palms to make a sausage shape of around 3½–¾in (8 x 2cm), tapering it slightly at each end. Fold each end of the roll in slightly to form a crescent shape. Line 2 baking sheets with parchment paper, and place the formed cookies on them, leaving a little space between each.

5 Bake the vanillekipferl at the top of the oven for 15 minutes, until they are very lightly colored. They should not brown at all.

6 Leave the cookies to cool on the sheets for 5 minutes, then transfer them to a wire rack. Scatter them liberally with confectioner's sugar, and leave them to cool completely.

STORE These will keep in an airtight container for 5 days.

BAKER'S TIP
A German Christmas tradition, these crescent-shaped cookies rely on the use of ground almonds for their delicate, crumbly texture. Many recipes recommend tossing the finished cookies in vanilla sugar, but if that proves difficult to find, the vanilla extract in the cookie dough will do just as well.

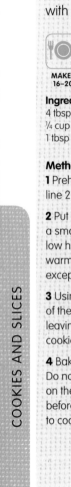

Florentines

These crisp Italian cookies are packed full of fruit and nuts, and coated with luxurious dark chocolate. Wonderful for a quick afternoon treat.

MAKES
16–20

20 MINS

15–20 MINS

Ingredients

4 tbsp butter
¼ cup sugar
1 tbsp honey
½ cup all-purpose flour, sifted
¼ cup chopped mixed peel
¼ cup glacé cherries, finely chopped
¼ cup blanched almonds, finely chopped
1 tsp lemon juice
1 tbsp heavy cream
6oz (175g) good-quality dark chocolate,
  broken into pieces

Method

1 Preheat the oven to 350°F (180°C) and line 2 baking sheets with parchment paper.

2 Put the butter, sugar, and honey into a small saucepan and melt gently over low heat. Then allow to cool until it is just warm. Stir in all the other ingredients except the chocolate.

3 Using a teaspoon, drop spoonfuls of the mixture onto the baking sheets, leaving space between them for the cookies to spread.

4 Bake for 10 minutes, or until golden. Do not let them get too dark. Leave them on the baking sheets for a few minutes before transferring them to a wire rack to cool completely.

5 Melt the chocolate pieces in a heatproof bowl set over a pan of gently simmering water. Make sure the bowl is not touching the water.

6 Once the chocolate has melted, use a palette knife to spread a thin layer of chocolate on the bottom of each cookie. Place the cookies chocolate-side up on a wire rack to set. Spread a second layer of chocolate over the cookies. Then just before they set, make a wavy line in the chocolate with a fork.

STORE These will keep in an airtight container for 5 days.

BAKER'S TIP

You can make a beautiful display of three different colors of Florentines by topping a third with milk chocolate, another third with white chocolate, and the remainder with dark chocolate. Or use different tones of chocolate both to top and to drizzle over in a zigzag fashion, for a stunning effect.

Biscotti

These crisp Italian biscuits make great presents, as they can be prettily packaged and will keep for days.

MAKES 25–30 | **15 MINS** | **40–45 MINS** | **UP TO 8 WEEKS**

Ingredients

1 cup whole almonds, skinned
1½ cups all-purpose flour
½ cup sugar
1 tsp baking powder
½ tsp salt
2 large eggs, at room temperature
1 tsp pure vanilla extract
4 tbsp unsalted butter, melted

1 Melt the butter in a small saucepan over low heat and then set aside to cool.

2 Preheat the oven to 350°F (180°C). Line a baking sheet with parchment paper.

3 Spread the almonds out on a non-stick baking sheet. Place in the center of the oven.

4 Bake the almonds for 5–10 minutes until slightly colored, tossing halfway.

5 Allow the almonds to cool until they are comfortable to handle. Coarsely chop them.

6 Sift the flour through a fine sieve held over a large bowl.

7 Add the sugar and chopped almonds to the bowl and stir until well combined.

8 In a separate bowl, whisk together the eggs, vanilla extract, and the melted butter.

9 Gradually pour the egg mixture into the flour while stirring with a fork.

10 Using your hands, bring the ingredients together to form a dough.

11 If the mixture seems too wet to shape easily, work in a little flour until it is pliable.

12 Turn the dough out onto a lightly floured work surface.

13 With your hands, form the dough into 2 log shapes, each about 8in (20cm) long.

14 Place on the lined baking sheet and bake for 20 minutes in the middle of the oven.

15 Remove the logs from the oven. Cool slightly, then transfer to a cutting board.

16 With a serrated knife, cut the logs diagonally into 1½–2in (3–5cm) thick slices.

17 Put the biscotti on a baking sheet and return to the oven for 10 minutes to dry even more.

18 Turn the biscotti with a palette knife, and return to the oven for another 5 minutes.

19 Cool the biscotti on a wire rack to harden them and allow any moisture to escape.

TO FREEZE Place the cooled biscotti on baking sheets and freeze until solid.

Transfer to freezer bags. **STORE** Keep unfrozen in an airtight container for over 1 week.

BISCOTTI

Biscotti variations

Hazelnut and Chocolate Biscotti

Add chocolate chips to the biscotti dough for a child-friendly alternative.

| MAKES 25–30 | 15 MINS | 40–45 MINS | UP TO 8 WEEKS |

Ingredients
1 cup whole hazelnuts, shelled
1½ cups all-purpose flour, sifted, extra for dusting
1 tsp baking powder
½ tsp salt
½ cup sugar
¼ cup dark chocolate chips
2 large eggs
1 tsp pure vanilla extract
4 tbsp unsalted butter, melted and cooled

Method
1 Preheat the oven to 350°F (180°C). Spread the nuts on a baking sheet. Bake for 5–10 minutes, tossing halfway through, until slightly colored. Cool, rub in a kitchen towel to remove excess skin, then coarsely chop.

2 In a bowl, mix together the flour, baking powder, salt, sugar, nuts, and chocolate chips. In a separate bowl, whisk the eggs, vanilla, and butter. Combine the wet and dry ingredients, mixing to form a dough. If the mixture is too wet, knead in a little extra flour to shape easily.

3 Put the dough onto a floured surface and form into 2 logs, each 8in (20cm) long by 3in (7cm). Place on a baking sheet lined with parchment paper and bake for 20 minutes in the middle of the oven. Take the logs out of the oven and allow them to cool slightly. Cut them diagonally into 1¼–2in (3–5cm) thick slices with a serrated knife.

4 Return the biscotti to the oven for another 15 minutes, turning after 10 minutes. They are ready when golden at the edges and hard to the touch. Cool the biscotti on a wire rack.

STORE These will keep in an airtight container for more than 1 week.

Chocolate and Brazil Nut Biscotti

These biscotti, darkened with cocoa powder, are ideal to serve after dinner with strong, black coffee.

| MAKES 25–30 | 15 MINS | 40–45 MINS | UP TO 8 WEEKS |

Ingredients
1 cup whole Brazil nuts, shelled
1⅓ cups all-purpose flour, sifted, extra for dusting
½ cup cocoa powder
½ cup sugar
1 tsp baking powder
½ tsp salt
2 large eggs
1 tsp pure vanilla extract
4 tbsp unsalted butter, melted and cooled

Method
1 Preheat the oven to 350°F (180°C). Spread the nuts on a baking sheet. Bake for 5–10 minutes. Cool slightly, rub in a kitchen towel to remove excess skin, then coarsely chop.

2 Mix the flour, cocoa powder, sugar, baking powder, salt, and nuts. In a separate bowl, whisk together the eggs, vanilla extract, and butter. Combine the wet and dry ingredients to form a dough.

3 Turn the dough out onto a floured surface and form 2 logs, each 8in (20cm) long by 3in (7cm). Place on a baking sheet lined with parchment paper and bake for 20 minutes. Cool slightly, then cut diagonally into 1¼–2in (3–5cm) thick slices with a serrated knife.

4 Return to the oven for 15 minutes, turning after 10, until golden and hard to the touch.

STORE These will keep in an airtight container for more than 1 week.

BAKER'S TIP
The hard, crunchy texture and toasted taste of biscotti is obtained by double-baking. This technique also allows them to keep well for a relatively long time.

Pistachio and Orange Biscotti

These fragrant biscotti are delicious served either with coffee or dipped in a glass of sweet dessert wine. ▶

| MAKES 25–30 | 15 MINS | 40–45 MINS | UP TO 8 WEEKS |

Ingredients
1 cup whole pistachios, shelled
1½ cups all-purpose flour, plus extra for dusting
½ cup sugar
finely grated zest of 1 orange
½ tsp baking powder
½ tsp salt
2 large eggs
1 tsp pure vanilla extract
4 tbsp unsalted butter, melted and cooled

Method
1 Preheat the oven to 350°F (180°C). Spread the pistachios on a baking sheet. Bake for 5–10 minutes. Cool, rub in a kitchen towel to remove excess skin, then coarsely chop.

2 In a bowl, mix the flour, sugar, zest, baking powder, salt, and nuts. In a separate bowl, whisk together the eggs, vanilla extract, and butter. Mix the wet and dry ingredients to form a dough.

3 Turn the dough out onto a floured surface and form into 2 logs, each 8in (20cm) long by 3in (7cm). Place them on a baking sheet lined with parchment paper and bake for 20 minutes in the middle of the oven. Cool slightly, then cut diagonally into ½in (1cm) thick slices with a serrated knife.

4 Bake for another 15 minutes, turning after 10, until golden and hard to the touch.

STORE These will keep in an airtight container for more than 1 week.

Shortbread

A Scottish classic, shortbread should only color very lightly in the oven, so remember to cover with foil if browning.

MAKES 8 WEDGES | **15 MINS** | **30–40 MINS**

Chilling time
1hr

Special equipment
8in (20cm) round cake pan

Ingredients
11 tbsp unsalted butter, softened,
  plus extra for greasing
⅓ cup sugar, plus extra for sprinkling
1⅓ cups all-purpose flour, plus extra
  for dusting
½ cup cornstarch

COOKIES AND SLICES

1 Preheat the oven to 325°F (160°C). Grease the pan and line with parchment paper.

2 Place the softened butter and sugar in a large bowl.

3 Cream together the butter and sugar with an electric hand mixer until light and fluffy.

4 Stir in the flour and cornstarch very gently, stopping as soon as the flours are mixed in.

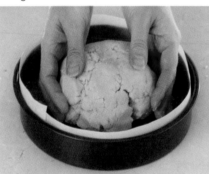

5 Bring together with your hands to form a rough, crumbly dough. Transfer to the pan.

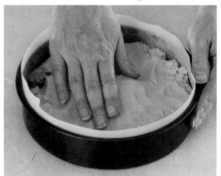

6 Firmly push the dough down with your hands to form a compact, even layer.

7 Score the circle of shortbread lightly, with a sharp knife, into 8 wedges.

8 Prick the shortbread all over with a fork to make a decorative pattern.

9 Cover the shortbread with plastic wrap and chill in the refrigerator for 1 hour.

10 Bake in the center of the oven for 30–40 minutes. Cover with foil if it browns quickly.

11 Take the shortbread out of the oven and re-score the wedges with a sharp knife.

12 While it is still warm, scatter a thin layer of sugar evenly over the top.

13 When cool, turn the shortbread gently out of its pan and break or cut it into wedges along the scored lines. **STORE** The shortbread will keep in an airtight container for 5 days.

Shortbread variations

Pecan Sandies

These addictive shortbread cookies are so-called because they are said to have the texture (though not the taste!) of fine sand.

MAKES 18–20 **15 MINS** **15 MINS**

Chilling time
30 mins (if needed)

Ingredients
7 tbsp unsalted butter, softened
¼ cup light brown sugar
¼ cup sugar
½ tsp pure vanilla extract
1 large egg yolk
1 cup all-purpose flour, sifted,
  plus extra for dusting
½ cup pecans, chopped

Method
1 Preheat the oven to 350°F (180°C). In a large bowl, cream together the butter and sugars with an electric hand mixer until light and fluffy. Add the vanilla extract and the egg yolk, and mix well to combine. Mix in the flour, then the pecans, and bring the ingredients together to form a rough dough.

2 Turn the dough out onto a lightly floured work surface and knead it to form a smooth dough. Roll into a log about 8in (20cm) long. If the dough seems too soft to cut, refrigerate it for 30 minutes to allow it to firm up.

3 Slice ½in (1cm) disks from the log, and place a little apart on 2 baking sheets lined with parchment paper. Bake in the top third of the oven for 15 minutes, until golden brown at the edges. Leave on the sheets for a few minutes, then transfer them to a wire rack to cool completely.

STORE The sandies will keep in an airtight container for 5 days.

Chocolate Chip Shortbread Cookies

Chocolate chips make these shortbread cookies child-friendly.

MAKES 14–16 **15 MINS** **15–20 MINS**

Ingredients
7 tbsp unsalted butter, softened
⅓ cup sugar
¾ cup all-purpose flour, sifted,
  plus extra for dusting
¼ cup cornstarch, sifted
¼ cup dark chocolate chips

Method
1 Preheat the oven to 340°F (170°C). In a large bowl with an electric hand mixer, cream together the butter and sugar until light and fluffy. Stir in the flour, cornstarch, and chocolate chips, and bring together to form a rough dough.

2 Turn the dough out onto a lightly floured work surface and gently knead it together until it becomes smooth. Roll into a 2½in (6cm) diameter log, and slice at ¼in (5mm) intervals into cookies. Place spaced apart on 2 non-stick baking sheets.

3 Bake in the center of the oven for about 15–20 minutes until lightly golden. They should not color too much. Leave on the sheets for a few minutes before transferring to a wire rack to cool completely.

STORE These will keep in an airtight container for 5 days.

Marbled Millionaire's Shortbread

A modern classic—extremely sweet and rich, just as it should be.

MAKES 16 SQUARES | **45 MINS** | **35–40 MINS**

Special equipment
8in (20cm) square cake pan

Ingredients
1½ cups all-purpose flour, plus more for dusting
12 tbsp unsalted butter, softened, plus extra for greasing
½ cup sugar

For the caramel filling
4 tbsp unsalted butter
¼ cup light brown sugar
14oz (400g) can condensed milk

For the chocolate topping
7oz (200g) milk chocolate
2 tbsp unsalted butter
2oz (50g) dark chocolate

Method
1 Preheat the oven to 325°F (160°C). Put the flour, butter, and sugar in a bowl and rub together to make crumbs. Grease the pan and dust with flour. Put the mixture into the pan and press it down with your hands until it is compact and even. Bake in the center of the oven for 35–40 minutes, until light golden brown. Leave to cool in the pan.

2 For the caramel, melt the butter and sugar in a heavy-bottomed saucepan over medium heat. Add the milk and bring to a boil, stirring constantly. Reduce the heat and cook on a steady simmer, still stirring constantly, for 5 minutes, until it thickens and darkens to a light caramel color. Pour the caramel over the cooled shortbread and leave to cool.

3 For the chocolate topping, put the milk chocolate and butter in a heatproof bowl over a pan of simmering water, without touching the water, until just melted. Stir well. Melt the dark chocolate without butter in a separate bowl in a similar way.

4 Pour the milk chocolate over the set caramel and smooth out. Pour the dark chocolate over the surface in a zigzag pattern and drag a fine skewer through the 2 chocolates to create a marbled effect. Leave to cool and harden before cutting into squares.

STORE These will keep in an airtight container for 5 days.

BAKER'S TIP
The secret to a good millionaire's shortbread is to make a caramel that sets enough so that it does not squish out of the sides on cutting, and a chocolate topping that is soft enough to cut easily. Add a little butter to the chocolate to soften it slightly, and gently cook the caramel until thickened to achieve a perfect result.

Flapjacks

These chewy bars are great energy boosters and very simple to make, using only a few pantry ingredients.

MAKES 16–20   **15 MINS**   **40 MINS**

Special equipment
10in (25cm) square
cake pan

Ingredients
16 tbsp butter, plus extra
  for greasing
1¼ cups light brown sugar
2 tbsp corn syrup
3¾ cups rolled oats

1 Preheat the oven to 300°F (150°C). Lightly grease the base and sides of the cake pan.

2 Put the butter, sugar, and syrup in a large saucepan and place over medium-low heat.

3 Stir constantly with a wooden spoon to prevent burning. Remove from the heat.

4 Stir in the oats, making sure they are well coated, but do not over-work the mix.

5 Spoon the oat mixture from the saucepan into the prepared pan.

6 Press down firmly with the wooden spoon to make a roughly even layer.

7 To neaten the surface, dip a tablespoon in hot water and use the back to smooth the top.

8 Bake for 40 minutes or until evenly golden; you may need to turn the pan in the oven.

9 Leave to cool for 10 minutes, then cut into 16 squares, or 20 rectangles, with a sharp knife.

10 Leave in the pan to cool completely, then lever the flapjacks out of the pan; a spatula is a useful tool for this.

STORE The flapjacks will keep in an airtight container for 1 week.

Flapjack variations

Hazelnut and Raisin Flapjacks

Hazelnuts and raisins make these a chewy and wholesome treat.

| MAKES 16–20 | 15 MINS | 30 MINS | UP TO 4 WEEKS |

Special equipment
8 x 10in (20 x 25cm) brownie pan, or similar

Ingredients
4 tbsp unsalted butter,
  plus extra for greasing
1¼ cups light brown sugar
2 tbsp corn syrup
3¾ cups rolled oats
⅔ cup chopped hazelnuts
¼ cup raisins

Method
1 Preheat the oven to 325°F (160°C). Grease the pan and line the base and sides with parchment paper. Melt the butter, sugar, and syrup in a heavy saucepan over low heat until the butter has melted. Remove the pan from the heat and stir in the oats, hazelnuts, and raisins.

2 Transfer the mixture to the prepared pan and press it down firmly, until it is compact and even. Bake in the center of the oven for 30 minutes until golden brown and darkening slightly at the edges.

3 Leave in the pan for 5 minutes, then cut the flapjacks into squares with a sharp knife. Leave in the pan until cold before turning out with a metal spatula.

STORE The flapjacks will keep in an airtight container for 1 week.

BAKER'S TIP
Nuts and raisins make these flapjacks healthier and, as in the recipes for Oat Cookies (see page 140), you could also add a handful of pumpkin or sunflower seeds. Despite the health quotient of those ingredients, the butter content of flapjacks does make them a high-fat treat.

Cherry Flapjacks

These cherry flapjacks have the perfect texture, and a delicious, toasty flavor. ▶

| MAKES 18 | 15 MINS | 25 MINS |

Chilling time
10 mins

Special equipment
8in (20cm) square cake pan

Ingredients
11 tbsp unsalted butter, plus extra for greasing
⅓ cup light brown sugar
2 tbsp corn syrup
3¾ cups rolled oats
1 cup glacé cherries, quartered, or ½ cup dried
  cherries, coarsely chopped
⅓ cup raisins
4oz (100g) white or milk chocolate,
  broken into small pieces, for drizzling

Method
1 Preheat the oven to 350°F (180°C). Lightly grease the cake pan. Place the butter, sugar, and syrup in a medium saucepan over low heat, and stir until melted. Remove from the heat, add the oats, cherries, and raisins, and stir until well mixed.

2 Transfer to the prepared pan and press down. Bake in the top of the oven for 25 minutes. Remove, cool slightly in the pan, then mark into 18 pieces with a knife.

3 When the flapjacks are cold, place the chocolate in a small heatproof bowl set over a saucepan of simmering water. Make sure the bowl does not touch the water. Drizzle the melted chocolate over the flapjacks using a teaspoon, then chill for about 10 minutes, or until the chocolate has set. Remove the block of flapjacks from the pan and cut into pieces as marked.

STORE The flapjacks will keep in an airtight container for 1 week.

Sticky Date Flapjacks

The quantity of dates in this recipe gives these flapjacks a toffee-like flavor and wonderfully moist consistency.

| MAKES 16 | 25 MINS | 40 MINS |

Special equipment
8in (20cm) square cake pan
blender

Ingredients
1½ cups pitted dates (Medjool are best), chopped
½ tsp baking soda
14 tbsp unsalted butter
1¼ cups light brown sugar
2 tbsp corn syrup
3⅓ cups rolled oats

Method
1 Preheat the oven to 325°F (160°C). Line the pan with parchment paper. Place the dates and baking soda in a pan with enough water to cover, simmer for 5 minutes, then drain, reserving the liquid. Purée in a blender with 3 tablespoons of cooking liquid. Set aside.

2 Melt the butter, sugar, and syrup together in a large pan, stirring to mix. Stir in the oats, then press half the mixture into the pan.

3 Spread the date purée over the top of the oats, then spoon the remaining oat mixture over the top. Bake for 40 minutes, or until golden brown. Leave to cool in the pan for 10 minutes, then cut into 16 squares with a knife. Leave to cool completely in the pan before serving.

STORE The flapjacks will keep in an airtight container for 1 week.

Chocolate and Hazelnut Brownies

The classic recipe, these brownies are moist and soft in the center and crisp on top.

MAKES 24 · **25 MINS** · **12–15 MINS**

Special equipment
9 x 13in (23 x 32cm) pan

Ingredients
1 cup hazelnuts
12 tbsp unsalted butter, diced
10oz (300g) dark chocolate (at least
  50 percent cocoa solids, or higher
  for more bitter brownies), chopped
1⅓ cups sugar
4 large eggs, beaten
1½ cups all-purpose flour
½ cup cocoa powder, extra to dust

1 Preheat the oven to 400°F (200°C). Scatter the hazelnuts evenly over a baking sheet.

2 Toast the nuts in the oven for 5 minutes until browned, being careful not to burn them.

3 Remove from the oven and rub the nuts in a kitchen towel to remove most of the skins.

4 Chop the hazelnuts coarsely—some big chunks and some small. Set aside.

5 Line the base and sides of the pan with parchment paper, allowing some overhang.

6 Put the chocolate and butter in a bowl set over simmering water, without touching the water.

7 Melt the chocolate and butter, stirring until smooth. Remove and leave to cool.

8 Once the mixture has cooled, mix in the sugar until very well blended.

9 Now add the eggs, 1 at a time, making sure each is well mixed before you add the next.

10 Sift in the flour and cocoa powder, lifting the sieve up high above the bowl to aerate.

11 Mix in the flour and cocoa until the batter is smooth and no patches of flour are seen.

12 Stir in the chopped nuts to evenly distribute them in the batter; the mixture should be thick.

13 Pour into the prepared pan and spread so the mixture fills the corners. Smooth the top.

14 Bake for 12–15 minutes, or until just firm to the touch on top and still soft underneath.

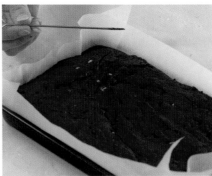

15 A skewer inserted should come out coated with a little batter. Remove from the oven.

16 Leave the brownie to cool completely in the pan to maintain the soft center.

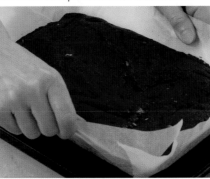

17 Lift the brownie from the pan using the edges of the paper to get a good grip.

18 Using a long, sharp, or serrated knife, score the surface of the brownie into 24 even pieces.

19 Boil some water in a saucepan and pour it into a shallow dish. Keep dish close at hand.

20 Cut the brownie into 24, wiping the knife between cuts and dipping it in the hot water.

21 Sift cocoa powder over brownies.
STORE Keep in an airtight container for 3 days.

Brownie variations

Sour Cherry and Chocolate Brownies

The sharp flavor and chewy texture of the dried sour cherries contrast wonderfully here with the rich, dark chocolate.

MAKES 16 | **15 MINS** | **20–25 MINS**

Special equipment
8in (20cm) square cake pan

Ingredients
11 tbsp unsalted butter, diced, extra for greasing
6oz (150g) good-quality dark chocolate
1¼ cups light brown sugar
1¼ cups all-purpose flour, plus extra for dusting
1¼ tsp baking powder
½ tsp salt
3 large eggs
1 tsp pure vanilla extract
½ cup dried sour cherries
4oz (100g) dark chocolate chunks

Method
1 Preheat the oven to 350°F (180°C). Grease the pan and dust with flour. Break up the chocolate and place with the butter in a heatproof bowl over simmering water, without touching the water, until just melted. Remove from the heat, add the sugar, and stir to combine. Cool slightly.

2 Sift the flour, baking powder, and salt into a separate bowl. Mix the eggs and vanilla extract into the chocolate mixture. Pour it into the flour and mix together. Be careful not to over-mix. Fold in the cherries and chocolate chunks.

3 Pour the mixture into the pan and bake in the center of the oven for 20–25 minutes. The brownies are ready when the edges are firm, but the middle is soft to the touch.

4 Cool in the pan for 5 minutes. Turn out and cut into squares. Cool further on a wire rack.

STORE The brownies will keep in an airtight container for 3 days.

BAKER'S TIP
The texture of a brownie is very much a matter of personal taste. Some people like them so squishy that they fall apart, others prefer a firmer cake. If you prefer soft brownies, reduce the cooking time slightly.

Walnut and White Chocolate Brownies

Slightly soft in the center, these make a tempting afternoon treat.

MAKES 16 | **10 MINS** | **1 HOUR 15 MINS**

Special equipment
8in (20cm) deep square pan

Ingredients
2 tbsp unsalted butter, diced, extra for greasing
2oz (50g) good-quality dark chocolate
3 large eggs
1 tbsp honey
1¼ cup light brown sugar
½ cup all-purpose flour
½ tsp baking powder
pinch salt
6oz (175g) walnut pieces
scant 1oz (25g) white chocolate, chopped

Method
1 Preheat the oven to 325°F (160°C). Lightly grease the pan, or line the base and sides with parchment paper.

2 Break the dark chocolate in pieces and put it with the butter into a heatproof bowl over a saucepan of simmering water until melted, stirring occasionally. Don't let the bowl touch the water. Remove the bowl from the pan and set aside to cool slightly.

3 Beat the eggs, honey, and sugar together, then gradually beat in the melted chocolate mixture. Sift the flour, baking powder, and salt over, add the walnuts and white chocolate, and fold in the ingredients. Pour the mixture into the prepared pan.

4 Put the pan in the oven and bake for 30 minutes. Cover loosely with foil and bake for another 45 minutes. The center should be a little soft. Leave to cool completely in the pan on a wire rack. When cold, turn out onto a board and cut into squares.

STORE The brownies will keep in an airtight container for 5 days.

White Chocolate Macadamia Blondies

A white chocolate version of the ever-popular brownie.

MAKES 24   **15 MINS**   **20 MINS**

Special equipment
8 x 10in (20 x 25cm) baking dish, or similar

Ingredients
10oz (300g) white chocolate, chopped
12 tbsp unsalted butter, diced, extra for greasing
1⅓ cups sugar
4 large eggs
1⅔ cups all-purpose flour, plus extra for dusting
1 cup macadamia nuts, coarsely chopped

Method
1 Preheat the oven to 400°F (200°C). Grease the pan and dust with flour. In a bowl set over a pan of simmering water, melt the chocolate and butter together, stirring now and again until smooth. Do not allow the bowl to touch the water. Remove and leave to cool for about 20 minutes.

2 Once the chocolate has melted, mix in the sugar (the mixture may well become thick and grainy, but the eggs will loosen the mixture). Using a balloon whisk, stir in the eggs 1 at a time, making sure each is well mixed in before you add the next. Sift in the flour, mix it in, then stir in the nuts.

3 Pour the mixture into the pan and gently spread it out into the corners. Bake for 20 minutes, or until just firm to the touch on top, but still soft underneath. Leave to cool completely in the pan, then cut into 24 squares, or fewer rectangles for bigger blondies.

STORE The blondies will keep in an airtight container for 5 days.

Index

About the author

After spending years as an international model, Caroline Bretherton dedicated herself to her passion for food, founding her company, Manna Food, in 1996.

Her fresh, light, and stylish cooking soon developed a stylish following to match, with a catering clientele that included celebrities, art galleries, theatres, and fashion magazines, as well as cutting edge businesses. She later expanded the company to include an all-day eatery called Manna Café on Portobello Road, in the heart of London's Notting Hill.

A move into the media has seen her working consistently in television over the years, guesting on and presenting a wide range of food programmes for terrestrial and cable broadcasters.

More recently Caroline has worked increasingly in print, becoming a regular contributor to *The Times on Saturday*, and writing her first book *The Allotment Cookbook.*

In her spare time, Caroline tends her beloved allotment near her home in London, growing a variety of fruits, vegetables, and herbs. When she can, she indulges her passion for wild food foraging, both in the city and the country.

She is married to Luke, an academic, and has two boys, Gabriel and Isaac, who were more than happy to test the recipes for this book.

Acknowledgments

The author would like to thank
Mary-Clare, Dawn, and Alastair at Dorling Kindersley for their help and encouragement with this massive task, as well as Borra Garson and all at Deborah McKenna for all their work on my behalf. Lastly I would like to thank all my family and friends for their tremendous encouragement and appetites!

Dorling Kindersley would like to thank
The following people for their work on the photoshoot:

Art Directors
Nicky Collings, Miranda Harvey, Luis Peral, Lisa Pettibone

Props Stylist
Wei Tang

Food Stylists
Kate Blinman, Lauren Owen, Denise Smart

Home Economist Assistant
Emily Jonzen

Baking equipment used in the step-by-step photography kindly donated by Lakeland. For all your baking needs contact: www.lakeland.co.uk; or order by phone on 015394 88100.

Caroline de Souza for art direction and setting the style of the presentation stills photography.

Dorothy Kikon for editorial assistance and Anamica Roy for design assistance.

Jane Ellis for proofreading and Susan Bosanko for indexing.

Thanks to the following people for their work on the US edition:

Consultant
Kate Curnes

Americanizers
Nichole Morford and Jenny Siklós

Thanks also to Steve Crozier for retouching.